The Data Storyteller's Handbook

The
Data
Storyteller's
Handbook

How to create **business impact** using data storytelling

Kat Greenbrook

First published in 2023
© 2023 by Kat Greenbrook, Aotearoa New Zealand
The Data Storyteller's Handbook, Kat Greenbrook

ISBN 978-0-473-69491-3 (Paperback)
ISBN 978-0-473-69493-7 (ePub)
ISBN 978-0-473-69494-4 (ePDF)

Created in conjunction with The Book Shelf Ltd.

roguepenguin.co.nz

This book is for anyone who has ever been asked to **"tell a story"** with their data.

Contents

Contents

Foreword

Once upon a time, there was a land filled with data. Countless analysts tried to tame the seemingly unending array of numbers, filling databases and spreadsheets and aggregating them into dashboards and reports. While these sensible structures helped, the quest to find meaning and convey insights continued. Years passed by. One day, an age-old concept came to the land: story. Those who learned to harness its magical power found their audiences captivated, recommendations followed, and careers propelled.

Whether you've been using this potent way to present data or this is your introduction to it, you're about to learn from an insightful data storyteller named Kat. Kat understands that— while it isn't advisable to begin your next board meeting or presentation with the phrase "Once upon a time..."–there *are* strategic and profound ways to use story in business. Clients, investors, executives, and other stakeholders all crave data. However, data, in isolation, lacks impact; it's the meaning we bring to it that drives comprehension, decisions, and action.

With this book, Kat has distilled her process for teaching people across industries and roles into a succinct and practical guide. Learn from the characters in each chapter as you connect with their relatable situations and challenges. Practice new approaches with the provided frameworks and worksheets. Apply the strategies shared to bring your data communications to a new level.

Finally, recognize that data stories are not just about numbers. They are about people. By placing the audience at the center of the narrative, Kat underscores the importance of empathy and connection in data communication. She reminds us that behind every interesting dataset is a tale waiting to be told— a narrative that can engage and enlighten.

The Data Storyteller's Handbook is an incredible resource that will inspire a new generation of storytellers to find enchantment in numbers and share their learnings with the world.

Cole Nussbaumer Knaflic

Bestselling author of *storytelling with data, let's practice!,* and *storytelling with you*

Introduction

**Do you work with data,
but struggle to explain to
others why it matters?**

Data is no longer reserved for specialists.

But simply having data isn't enough. If you want to be a data-driven business, it's important for decision-makers to understand the significance of data insights.

Data storytelling communicates business stories using the language of data insights. It serves as a bridge, connecting the world of data analytics with the realm of business stakeholders.

This book is for anyone who has to communicate data.

It's your ultimate business guide to data storytelling.

Whether you're a data analyst, business leader, marketer, researcher, accountant, or anyone else working with data–this book is for you. While you may not aspire to be an expert Data Storyteller, you recognise the significance of this skill in achieving your goals.

Designed for busy professionals, it's the perfect resource to enhance data communication skills quickly.

PROBLEMS

Are there times when your explanation of data insight leaves others confused?

Do you find it challenging to hold the attention of your audience when presenting data?

Do you feel stakeholders don't support your work because they don't understand the impact it could create?

SOLUTION

Use effective data storytelling to better communicate your data insights.

BENEFITS

Achieve business goals
Data storytelling enables many data-driven business actions.

Enhance decision-making
Data storytelling leads to more informed and empathetic decision-making.

Engage people with data
Data storytelling communicates data in a way that resonates with a specific audience.

Increase data literacy and business acumen
Data storytelling enhances an audience's understanding of both data insights and business concepts.

This book enables you to be a skilled Data Storyteller.

This book is your illustrated guide for using data storytelling to communicate. It's based on a proven workshop structure and takes a practical approach to the data storytelling process. It will equip you with the knowledge, tools, and mindset you need to become a master of data storytelling.

As your time is valuable, diving into a dense, in-depth text might not be your top priority. That's why this book provides concise, illustrated, and actionable guidance you can put into practice immediately. You'll feel empowered to turn (what some might see as boring) data into a compelling story that truly makes an impact.

This is not another data visualisation book.

As more people work with data, many are recognising the importance of data communication skills. But data storytelling is a hard skill to master if you don't understand what it is or how to get started.

When you're learning, it's important to differentiate between data storytelling and data visualisation—they are not always the same thing.

So, while this book talks a bit about data visualisation, it's not primarily a data visualisation book. This book will teach you not only what data storytelling is, but also how to do it.

DATA STORYTELLING COMMUNICATES A DATA-DERIVED MESSAGE.

THIS MAY OR MAY NOT BE VISUAL.

DATA VISUALISATION PRESENTS DATA VISUALLY.

THIS MAY OR MAY NOT TELL A STORY.

This book doesn't cover *everything*.

What this book covers will enable you to become a better Data Storyteller. But there are things it doesn't cover (for good reason), which you may be expecting it to.

- **This book won't teach you how to analyse data.** Data analysis happens before data storytelling (or at least it should!). This book focuses on how to communicate the insights gained from data analysis using data storytelling.

- **This book won't teach you data visualisation best practices.** Best-practice data visualisation is a whole book on its own. This book focuses on how to use data visualisations to communicate your data story.

- **This book won't teach you how to design a dashboard.** In my opinion, dashboards aren't data storytelling tools. Unlike data storytelling, they don't communicate a specific message, but rather present data for an already knowledgeable audience to interpret.

- **This book will teach you to understand how the work you do contributes to business success.** This understanding helps you better communicate, collaborate, and influence within the business.

- **This book will teach you how to understand (and build more empathy) for your audience.** Data communication is a two-way street, so considering your audience will help make your data storytelling resonate.

- **This book will teach you how to find story building blocks from your data analysis.** Data analysis uncovers many stories, but understanding what data is part of what story will help you communicate a clear message.

- **This book will teach you how to write an engaging and compelling data narrative.** Data storytelling weaves data into a narrative of context and explanation.

- **This book will teach you how to communicate your data story using visuals.** Data storytelling visuals are usually *less* focused on aesthetics and *more* focused on how effectively they communicate a message.

CHAPTER BREAKDOWN

Know

Chapter 1: Why Visualise Your Data?

Chapter 2: Why Tell Stories with Your Data?

How

Chapter 3: The Business
Why do you want to communicate?

Chapter 4: The Audience
Whom will you communicate with?

Chapter 5: The Data Story
What is your message?

Chapter 6: The Telling
How will you communicate
your data story?

Do

Chapter 7: The Practice

Feel free to jump around in this book.

You don't have to read this book from cover to cover.

While I suggest starting with the first two chapters to get some context, feel free to mix it up and explore the chapters that catch your attention. It's a journey. Make it your own!

If you're a fan of skim reading, you're in luck. This book is designed with your reading style in mind. Simply flip through the pages, and you'll discover something interesting.

Who am I to write this book?

Kia ora / Hi. My name is Kat.

I live in New Zealand, work as a Data Storyteller, and am easily annoyed by unclear data visuals. I also buy books with the hope of magically absorbing the content. This book is a product of all the above.

I spent the first ten years of my career in different analytics roles—Reporting Analyst, Insight Analyst, Data Scientist. But the deeper I delved into data, the more disheartened I became. I saw such a disconnect between data and business teams. It was frustrating to work hard on building an analytical model to have it not be used. So, I hatched an escape plan and got a degree in graphic design—"maybe, I could be a graphic designer?"

But the universe had other ideas. It countered my decision to leave the data space, with the rise of the data visualisation field. And this is a field I leaned into—hard. I saw data visuals as a way to engage others with analytics—"maybe, if my data looked good, it would get noticed?"

And it did get noticed, at least for a few minutes. My visuals grabbed initial interest, but this faded when the design appreciation wore off. I learned good design alone won't make data resonate with others. Something was missing… and that something was the magical buzzword "story".

In 2016, I established the data storytelling company Rogue Penguin (before you ask, yes, there are real penguins in New Zealand). Rogue Penguin exists to help business professionals communicate data insights.

This book is the result of hundreds of data storytelling workshops, along with years of refining content and techniques. It represents the very best of what I've learned and witnessed. I hope this book helps you on your data storytelling journey.

CHAPTER 1

Why Visualise Your Data?

To understand

Data storytelling is different from data visualisation.

Data visuals might be involved in data storytelling, but not all data visuals are created to tell stories.

It's important to understand how data visualisation fits into the data storytelling process. This chapter describes the three main reasons a business visualises data.

Data Visualisation

Data visualisation existed before you did.

Despite its widespread use today, data visualisation actually dates back hundreds of years. Maps are some of our oldest data visuals used by explorers to navigate, mark ownership, and record the locations of geological resources.

It wasn't until the 1800s that data visuals began to resemble the graphs we see today. Graphs became popular as governments and businesses collected and needed to analyse more and more data.

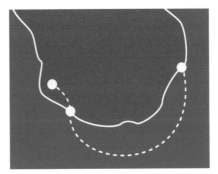

Florence Nightingale was a British nurse sent to the Crimean War in 1854. On arrival at the military hospital, she saw more soldiers suffering from disease (caused by poor hospital conditions) than from their battle wounds. Florence set about establishing good medical and hygiene practices—but it wasn't until a broken sewer was repaired that death rates began to improve.

When she returned to England two years later, Florence was determined to help improve military healthcare. She had kept detailed records of soldier illness and deaths, and knew this data could provide the evidence leaders needed to create change.

To help both the government and public understand the data, Florence created visualisations to show the impact improved sanitation had on death rates (they fell by 95%!). Her work publicised the army's healthcare failings and highlighted an urgent need for change. Many improvements were made, based on Florence's data analysis and visual communication.

Businesses typically visualise data for three reasons.

Data visualisation began as a relatively simple field—visualising data made it easy to analyse. But as data became a key part of business operations, visuals went from being an analytics tool to also being an effective way to share insight.

Today, some are used as tools to discover data insights, while others have become a form of modern communication.

In business, the three main reasons to visualise data are to **Discover**, to **Inform**, or to **Educate**.

3 REASONS TO VISUALISE DATA

DISCOVER

I want to **discover** insights in my data.

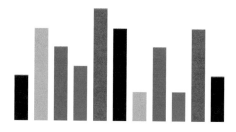

INFORM

I want to **inform** others of my data.

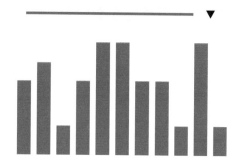

EDUCATE

I want to **educate** others about my data.

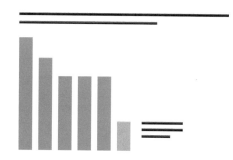

Your reason to visualise data is a separate decision to the chart type you use.

Sometimes, you'll use the <u>same</u> chart type to **Discover**, **Inform**, and **Educate**.

And sometimes, you'll use <u>different</u> chart types to **Discover**, **Inform**, and **Educate**.

Your choice of chart type should be based on your data or your audience (usually both). For example, you might be comfortable using a complex chart type to analyse data (**Discover**) but then need a more familiar chart type to communicate it (**Inform** or **Educate**).

REASON IS INDEPENDENT OF CHART TYPE

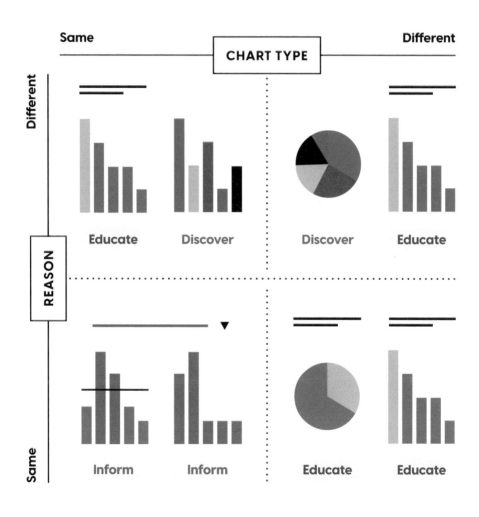

Not all data visuals are created to tell stories.

Data storytelling is used when you want to **Educate** your audience. However, it's still important to know how visuals to **Discover** and **Inform** relate to the data storytelling process.

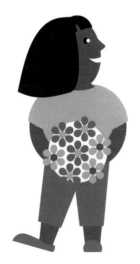

Visualising Data
to Discover

CURIOSITY KILLED THE CAT, BUT SATISFACTION BROUGHT IT BACK.
IGGY POP

When analysing data, visuals help you discover insights.

Discover data visuals aren't designed to be shared. You are their primary audience, so focus on how they can help you analyse the data. Don't worry if they look messy or break data visualisation "rules".

Discover data visuals are often created in large quantities and associated with the term "chart vomit". Don't let this label stop you from using them.

ANATOMY OF A DISCOVER VISUAL

Bakery sales

There is no wrong way to design Discover visuals.

Number

— Online
— In-store
— Wholesale
— Catering

Revenue

.... Online
.... In-store
.... Wholesale
.... Catering

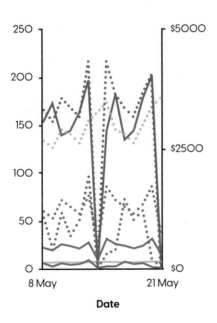

Date

ARE YOU COMMUNICATING DATA?

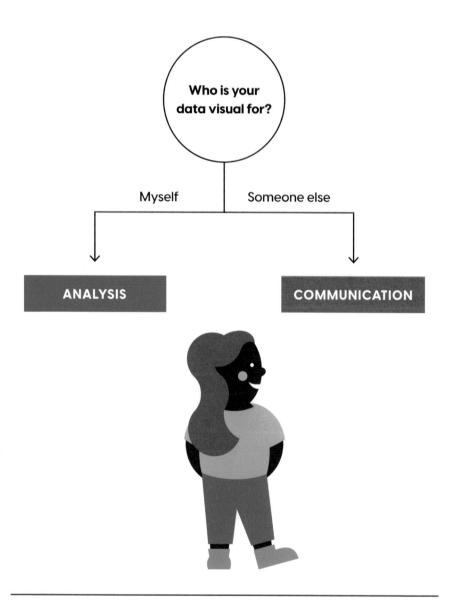

A DATA VISUAL DESIGNED FOR SOMEONE ELSE IS A FORM OF COMMUNICATION.

DISCOVER VISUALS PLAY AN IMPORTANT ROLE IN THE ANALYTICS PROCESS, BUT THEY ARE **NOT** A FORM OF DATA COMMUNICATION, BECAUSE THEY ARE DESIGNED ONLY FOR YOU.

Keep your Discover visuals for yourself.

Discover visuals are part of the analysis process and aren't designed to be shared (unless you're also sharing the analysis with someone). These visuals help you see patterns and discover insights.

The next step is to share those insights by using either an **Inform** or **Educate** visual. Before sharing, pause for a moment and make sure your information is accurate.

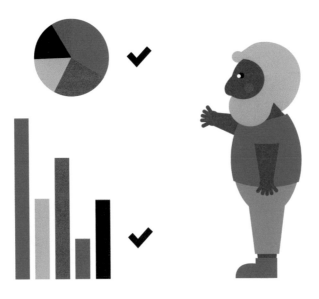

Visualising Data to Inform

A ROOSTER CROWS ONLY WHEN IT SEES THE LIGHT. PUT HIM IN THE DARK AND HE'LL NEVER CROW.
MUHAMMAD ALI

Inform visuals make data easy to view and access.

A good example of **Inform** visuals is the graphs included in dashboards. These graphs show specific metrics, arranged in an ordered way, so users can quickly understand the latest data.

It can be hard for people to access and understand data for a number of reasons. Accessing the data system might be difficult or require specialised knowledge or tools, or it might be that the good data is surrounded by lots of other data that isn't important, creating "data noise".

Both complicated systems and data noise create barriers to accessing data. **Inform** visuals help address these issues.

ANATOMY OF AN INFORM VISUAL

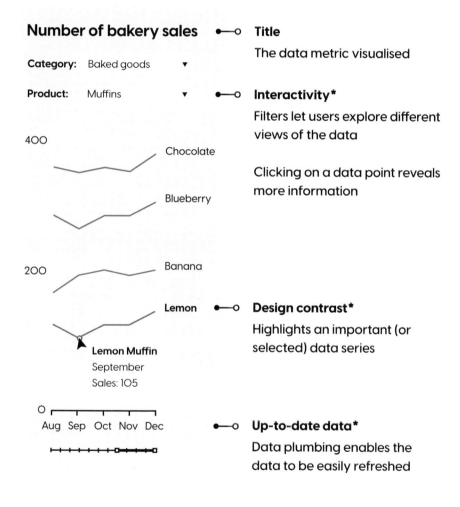

Number of bakery sales

Category: Baked goods ▾

Product: Muffins ▾

400

Chocolate

Blueberry

200

Banana

Lemon

Lemon Muffin
September
Sales: 105

Aug Sep Oct Nov Dec

Title
The data metric visualised

Interactivity*
Filters let users explore different views of the data

Clicking on a data point reveals more information

Design contrast*
Highlights an important (or selected) data series

Up-to-date data*
Data plumbing enables the data to be easily refreshed

* optional

Don't <u>overestimate</u> your audience.

While **Inform** visuals present data clearly, they don't explain what the data means. It's important not to assume your audience is familiar with the data or topic. I talk more about this in **Chapter 4: The Audience**.

If you think your audience needs more context, an **Educate** visual may be more suitable.

TO ENSURE YOUR AUDIENCE UNDERSTANDS YOUR DATA, YOU FIRST NEED TO UNDERSTAND YOUR AUDIENCE.

WHAT'S YOUR REASON TO VISUALISE DATA?

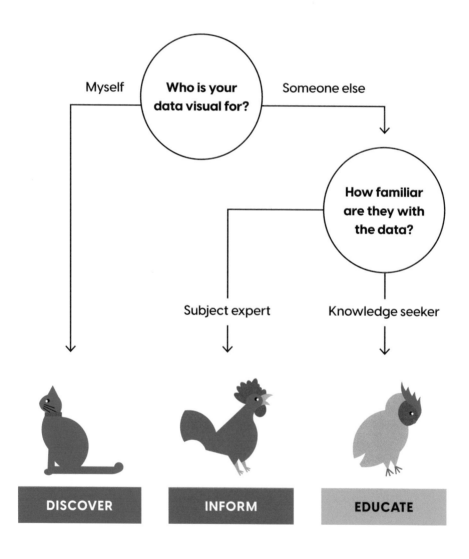

Visualising Data to Educate

THERE'S ALWAYS A HIDDEN OWL IN KNOWLEDGE.
E. I. JANE

Educate visuals explain the meaning of data.

Educate visuals don't just show an audience the data (like an **Inform** visual); they tell the audience what it means. To do that, they need to include a story.

The biggest difference between **Educate** and **Inform** visuals is the presence (or absence) of a story.

ONLY EDUCATE VISUALS NEED A STORY

	Consider your audience	Identify your data story
DISCOVER	✕	✕
INFORM	✓	✕
EDUCATE	✓	✓

Educate visuals are how you tell a data story.

Educate visuals are found in many forms of business communication, including reports, infographics, and presentations.

Educate visuals are covered more in **Chapter 6: The Telling**.

YOU CAN'T DESIGN EDUCATE VISUALS WITHOUT FIRST UNDERSTANDING THE DATA STORY.

ANATOMY OF AN EDUCATE VISUAL

Data story (covered in **Chapter 5: The Data Story**)

A data story is a narrative that explains the data's meaning to an audience. It helps to outline the bigger picture. Here's an example of a data story:

> **Sweet Delights** is a family-owned and operated bakery. They were established over 30 years ago and have a strong local reputation. But recently, after another bakery opened nearby, Sweet Delights' sales began to drop. So, to win back customers, their team launched a successful loyalty program.

Emotive elements

Images, colours, or words can be used to emotionally connect an audience with what the data represents.

Educate visual

This graph supports all—or part—of the data story.

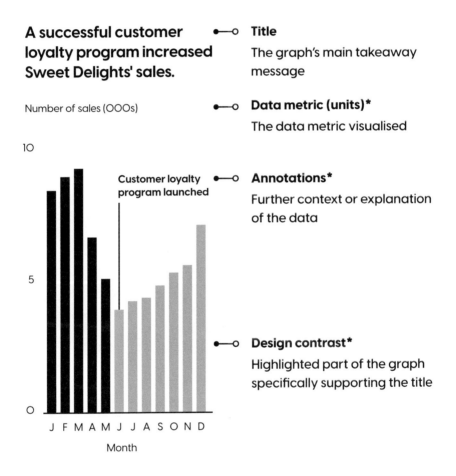

A successful customer loyalty program increased Sweet Delights' sales.

●—○ **Title**
The graph's main takeaway message

Number of sales (OOOs)

●—○ **Data metric (units)***
The data metric visualised

Customer loyalty program launched

●—○ **Annotations***
Further context or explanation of the data

●—○ **Design contrast***
Highlighted part of the graph specifically supporting the title

J F M A M J J A S O N D

Month

* optional

Recognise when a data visual needs to tell a story.

You don't have to tell a story every time you communicate data. Before learning the data storytelling process, it's important to understand when you'll need to use it.

To Inform or to Educate?

Data visuals don't usually exist in isolation.

When communicating data to others, you'll need to choose between creating an **Inform** or **Educate** visual. In practice, you'll usually create multiple visuals.

Inform visuals are usually grouped to create a **Dashboard**.

Educate visuals are usually grouped to tell a **Data Story**.

MULTIPLE VISUALS ARE COMMON

A **Dashboard** is created using multiple **Inform** visuals.

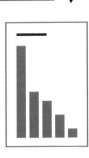 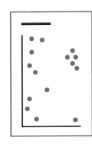 

A **Data Story** can be told using multiple **Educate** visuals.

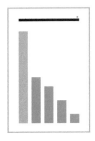 

Be clear on your data communication goals.

To decide whether you need an **Inform** or an **Educate** visual, think about what you want to achieve.

Providing either too little (or too much) context can get in the way of an audience's understanding of data. If your audience is familiar with the data, an **Inform** visual should be fine—but if they're not, an **Educate** visual will help guide their understanding.

If you want your audience to take a specific action or understand a specific message, an **Inform** visual (presenting data without context or explanation) probably isn't enough, and you'll need to create an **Educate** visual.

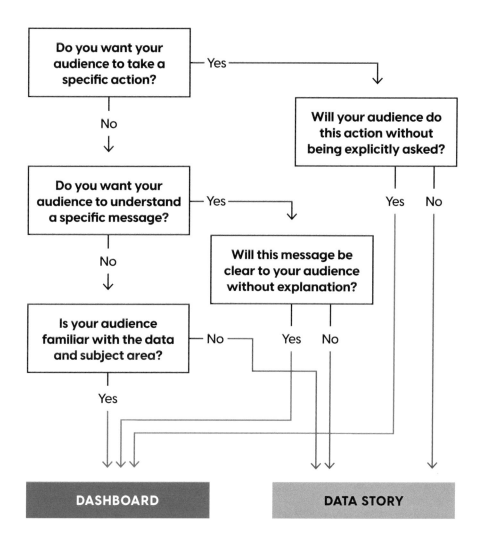

A DASHBOARD IS CREATED TO INFORM.

A DATA STORY IS CREATED TO EDUCATE.

A DASHBOARD IS NOT A DATA STORY.

Mistakes to Avoid

Mistake Number 1: Sharing Discover Visuals

These visuals are designed as a tool to help you analyse data but they're not a form of data communication and aren't meant to be shared. Although these visuals make sense to you (as the person who analysed the data), they are unlikely to be easily understood by others.

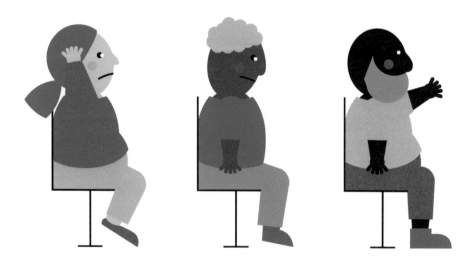

Sam is a Finance Analyst at a small boutique bank.

Recently, he analysed the credit risk of bank customers. Excited to share his findings with his wider team, Sam presented his Discover visuals during a meeting. He knew they weren't pretty, but thought they still clearly showed the important information.

Sam began to present his data... then, mid-presentation, he had a horrible feeling of regret.

He realised that what had been obvious to him (after going through the analysis process) was less obvious to his colleagues. Sam assumed the team would understand the visuals without further explanation.

After reflecting on the meeting, Sam now designs visuals for his audience (not himself) when presenting data.

Mistake Number 2: Overestimating Your Audience

When communicating data (and choosing whether to create an **Inform** or **Educate** visual), you need to know what your audience understands. If you present information that is too advanced for your audience, you will lose their attention. So, start with what they already know. This is covered further in **Chapter 4: The Audience**.

Use an **Inform** visual for an audience of subject experts or an **Educate** visual for an audience seeking to learn.

Ari is a Reporting Analyst at an insurance company.

After building a new financial dashboard, he was excited to be asked to share this with the marketing team. He was proud of what he had created.

All eyes were on Ari as he began to present his dashboard. His presentation focused on what he found most interesting—the technology. Ari had spent weeks working on the interactivity and data drill-downs. He wanted to show this functionality off.

One by one, his audience's eyes glazed over. He knew they had stopped listening. When his presentation was over, the only questions Ari got were about the data's significance. He felt frustrated.

Ari had assumed the marketing team had the same level of data knowledge he did, but they didn't. Therefore, they couldn't appreciate his dashboard's potential because they didn't understand the meaning of the data in it.

DATA CONTEXT IS HOW YOU FRAME THE MEANING OF YOUR NUMBERS AROUND THE KNOWLEDGE OF YOUR AUDIENCE.

The Pathways of Data Insights

THE DATA INSIGHT PATHWAYS

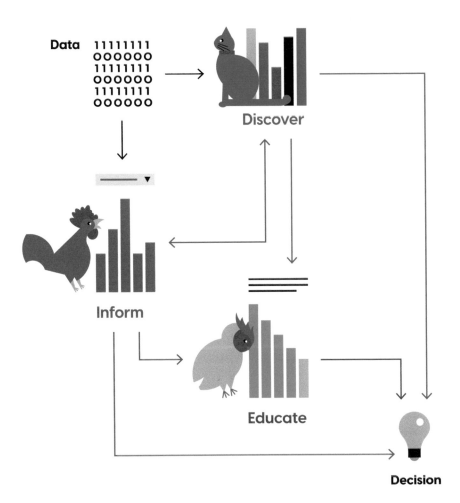

The three reasons to visualise data (to Discover, to Inform, and to Educate) work together within the insight pathway.

In a large organisation, there's a high chance you'll need to visualise your data in multiple ways. Before creating a data visual, know your reason and audience.

You might create **Discover** visuals to understand the data, then present the key metrics as **Inform** visuals in a dashboard. In time, these metrics might be important for non-subject experts, so you'll create **Educate** visuals for them and tell a data story.

It's okay to visualise the same data differently—in fact, it's recommended!

Michelle is a Pricing Analyst at a large energy retailer. She helps others make informed decisions about pricing strategies.

When analysing data, Michelle creates lots of Discover visuals. They're one of her favourite things to make because it doesn't matter what they look like. They're for her eyes only. These visuals help her identify patterns and trends.

When she understands the key metrics, Michelle creates Inform visuals (as part of a dashboard) that she shares with business experts. These visuals make it easy for others to understand and act upon the data.

Senior leaders also need to understand the metrics. So, Michelle creates Educate visuals for them to help her communicate a data story.

Through the use of Discover, Inform, and Educate visuals, Michelle plays a vital role in decisions that shape the energy retailer.

Whom Are You Visualising Data For?

DISCOVER VISUALS ARE DESIGNED FOR THEIR **CREATOR.**

INFORM VISUALS ARE DESIGNED FOR THEIR AUDIENCE.

EDUCATE VISUALS ARE DESIGNED FOR THEIR **CREATOR...**

...AND THEIR **AUDIENCE**.

Not all data visuals are designed to tell data stories.

Understanding your reason to visualise data helps determine whether you need a data story.

If you know you're using **Discover** visuals as part of your analytics process, you don't need to worry about data storytelling—yet.

If you know your audience will understand an **Inform** visual as part of a dashboard, you don't need to worry about data storytelling—yet.

But if you know your audience will struggle to understand the significance of data without explanation, then you'll need to use data storytelling. Identifying that is a valuable starting point for your data storytelling project.

CONSIDER THE **FUNCTION** OF YOUR DATA VISUAL BEFORE DESIGNING ITS **FORM**.

CHAPTER 2

Why Tell Stories with Your Data?

To educate

Data storytelling is a *process*.

The data storytelling process happens after the data analytics process. A data story is an effective way to communicate insights found from data analysis.

Even though this is not a data analysis book, it's important to acknowledge that the integrity of data storytelling relies on the robustness of the preceding data analysis.

The Act of Data Storytelling

"Tell me a data story"... Eeeeek!

Do you feel uncomfortable when someone asks you to make your data tell a story? You may associate storytelling with words like "fictional", "emotional", or "creative" and wonder how they relate to talking about data.

The term "storytelling" has been adopted by many fields, and what it means to tell a story has evolved. Storytelling in business is different from storytelling in the film industry, which is different again from fine arts storytelling.

Unlike the *film* industry, business stories aren't fictional. They're usually driven by the insights gained through data analysis.

Unlike *fine art* storytelling, business stories aren't subjective. They clearly state what the audience needs to understand.

Despite these differences, all storytelling has one thing in common: it's a form of communication to evoke an emotion or action.

Data storytelling communicates business stories.

Think of data as a language used in most businesses to describe operations or strategy.

Within a business, some teams may speak different data languages. For example, someone working in finance might not understand customer-service data metrics, and vice versa. Occasionally, you might need to share data with people who don't speak or use your terminology.

Storytelling can help improve data communication between teams. The more you communicate your insights using storytelling, the more you help grow the data literacy and business acumen of your audience.

Storytelling also helps improve data communication with customers. It lets you tell business stories in a way that can resonate with customers and build brand loyalty.

Swati is a Marketing Coordinator at a retail chain.

Every quarter, the company's Data and Analytics team presents their work to the wider business. Swati dreaded it. It's not that she doesn't like data—she uses data in her role. But the team's presentations have always left her feeling out of her depth. She was sure this presentation would be no different. She sat back, resigned, as Ricardo (a Data Analyst) began to speak.

To her surprise, Ricardo had Swati's full attention. Instead of talking about data, he described a common business problem—one Swati was personally struggling with. Ricardo never mentioned how he had analysed the data (something Swati found boring). His talk focused on customers, and any data he presented supported his story.

Ricardo's presentation left Swati energised. She felt a renewed sense of engagement with the business and an increased understanding of its data. Swati was excited to apply what she'd learnt from Ricardo's data insights to her own work.

Be Led by Your Data (Don't Lead It)

Good data analysis fuels good data stories.

You can't communicate data insights if the data hasn't been analysed. You don't need to have personally done the analysis, but as the person responsible for communicating it, you should understand its implications (and limitations).

It's okay to have an idea of the story before analysing the data, like having a hypothesis before conducting an experiment. But this story idea shouldn't make you analyse your data differently. You shouldn't <u>cherry-pick</u> your data, which means selecting data points that support a predetermined story while ignoring those that don't.

So, while it's great to start with questions that you want to answer through analysis, don't start with a fixed story—let the data lead you to that.

DON'T CHERRY-PICK YOUR DATA

The right order of events

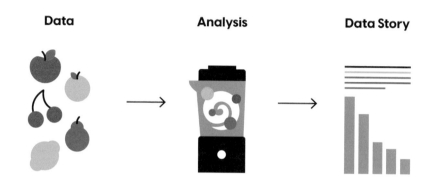

Data   Analysis   Data Story

The wrong order of events

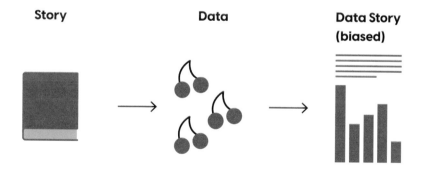

Story   Data   Data Story (biased)

DATA ANALYSIS MAKES OR BREAKS A DATA STORY.

DON'T SKIP THE DATA ANALYTICS PROCESS.

Not Every Data Story Needs a Data Visual

A data story can be visual, verbal, or written.

There are many data visualisation tools available today that allow you to cut up and view your data in whichever way you like.

However, not every data story will include visuals. You could tell a good data story while waiting in line for a coffee. The most effective data stories communicate the meaning of data to their audience in a variety of ways.

The benefit of using a visual is that it can imprint an image on your audience, making it easier for them to retain your message. These are covered more in **Chapter 6: The Telling**.

DATA STORYTELLING IS LESS ABOUT THE TOOL YOU USE AND MORE ABOUT THE PROCESS YOU FOLLOW.

Kofi is a Data Scientist at a software company.

After analysing customer purchases, Kofi created a model to try to predict what an individual customer would buy next. He was invited to present his work to senior leaders. They wanted to understand how the business was using data science. Kofi was nervous about the presentation and put a lot of work into creating his slides.

As he arrived at the meeting room, Kofi felt his stomach hit the floor. There was no screen or projector. His slides were useless. After an initial panic, Kofi decided to focus on his message. He knew how his work impacted the business. He knew what data insights he had discovered. He didn't need visuals to communicate this.

Kofi nailed the meeting. As a bonus, he sent his visuals to everyone afterwards to provide more detail. On reflection, Kofi wondered if his detailed slides might have actually been more distracting than helpful.

Data Storytelling Enables Better Decisions

Data storytelling enables *data-informed* decisions.

Effective data communication is essential in business, and storytelling is a powerful way to achieve this.

Many businesses spend millions on data analytics, dashboard reporting tools, and teams of people to operate these tools. While these investments are important, their value will only be realised if the insights from the data are communicated clearly.

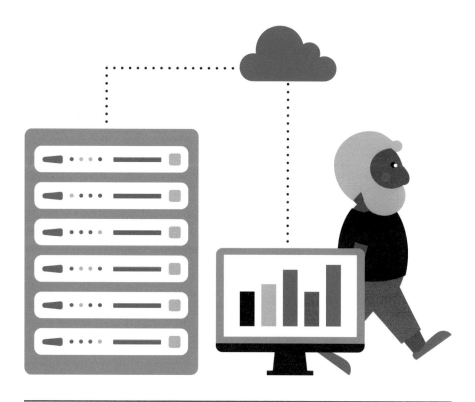

Tania is a Digital Analyst at a clothing retailer.

She was relatively new to the business and responsible for monitoring the performance of the website. Tania was also excited to make her mark and always looking for ways to enhance the customer experience.

One of the first things Tania noticed about the website was that its conversion rate was low (compared to the industry average). She knew she could improve it... but had to justify the budget. Tania wanted to A/B test various web pages and needed help from a website developer whom the business would need to pay for.

So, Tania used data storytelling to influence her manager. She highlighted the potential extra sales revenue a higher conversion rate would generate and how this would cover the initial cost of a developer within three months.

Tania got the go-ahead for her testing. Her work increased the website's conversion rate and future sales.

Data storytelling enables more *empathic* decisions.

Data storytelling uses narrative and emotive design elements (such as images, words, and colours) to create more powerful communication. It helps decision-makers gain a deeper understanding of the implications behind the numbers.

A graph alone (made up of unemotive shapes and lines) will often fail to capture the human experience of the data it visualises. As people become increasingly detached from the reality behind the data, it's harder for them to empathise.

Jeff is a Wildlife Conservation Scientist at a government department.

While analysing data, he observed a decline in the population of kororā (little blue penguins) caused by increased dog attacks. Jeff collected more data on the overall harm these attacks caused to the kororā colonies. He also gathered personal stories from community members who had witnessed the attacks.

Jeff met with government decision-makers and representatives from local councils and animal control agencies. To raise awareness, he used data storytelling to emphasise both the data insights and the vulnerability of the kororā population.

His approach led decision-makers to recognise the need for immediate action. Together, they targeted a campaign for dog owners, with incentives for responsible behaviour. Fenced areas and signage around kororā habitats were set up to prevent further harm. Jeff felt proud of his part in helping protect future kororā populations.

DATA STORYTELLING ENABLES MORE DATA-INFORMED AND EMPATHIC DECISIONS.

The Six Ws of
Data Storytelling

The six Ws framework for data storytelling.

The six Ws (**W**hy, **W**ho, **W**hat, Ho**w**, **W**hen, and **W**here) have traditionally been used in journalism to craft a good story. Despite centuries passing, these story elements remain popular in modern journalism.

The six Ws are also commonly used in business to gather project information—so it's only fitting they can also inform your data storytelling process.

You can either answer all six Ws before starting your data storytelling process or work through them in the following order:

1. **Why** do you want to communicate?
2. **Whom** will you communicate with?
3. **What** is your message?
4. **How** will you communicate your message?
5. **When** will you share your communication?
6. **Where** will you share your communication?

Jeff's Data Storytelling Ws

Remember Jeff?

Below are six data storytelling Ws related to his project on page 89.

Why	Raise awareness of Kororā (little blue penguin) population decline
Who	Local councils and animal control agencies
What	Kororā populations are threatened due to an increase in dog attacks
How	Visual slide presentation
When	Friday 1pm
Where	Council office

The following four chapters cover the Why, Who, What, and How of the data storytelling process.

The last two Ws (When and Where) are determined by the preferences of the Data Storyteller and their audience.

DATA ANALYTICS PROCESS

DATA STORYTELLING PROCESS

Why: The Business

Why do you want to communicate?

Who: The Audience

Whom will you communicate with?

What: The Data Story

What is your message?

How: The Telling

How will you communicate your message?

Why: The Business

Why do you want to communicate?

It's hard to tell an effective data story without understanding the business it represents. You need to be clear about what your data storytelling will help the business achieve and what impact it can create.

Chapter 3: The Business has advice on how you can use data storytelling to create business impact.

Who: The Audience

Whom will you communicate with?

It's important to understand the needs and motivations of your audience.

Chapter 4: The Audience has tools to help you build empathy for your audience.

What: The Data Story

What is your message?

Writing a data story is an exercise in clear and structured business communication.

Chapter 5: The Data Story has frameworks to help you identify and arrange your insights into a narrative structure.

How: The Telling

How will you communicate your message?

Data stories can be told visually, verbally, or in writing. This book focuses on visual methods.

Chapter 6: The Telling highlights some of the <u>visual</u> ways you can communicate a data story to your audience.

Respect the order of the Ws.

The data storytelling process is easier when you understand why you're communicating and whom you're communicating with. It's also easier to tell a data story when you've worked out what you want to say. So, write the data story first and then tell it (possibly using visuals).

Understanding the business and audience is the more strategic aspect of the data storytelling process, so don't overlook it.

Keep It Honest

Ethics matter in data storytelling.

Data storytelling is a relatively new field, blending the practices of other fields, such as data, analytics, communication, and design.

Each of those fields has unique ethical considerations. For example, when you work in communication, you should consider what your motivation is for sharing a specific message. Do your personal views bias your message?

At the end of upcoming chapters in this book, you'll find a **Keep It Honest** section with questions designed to help you maintain integrity in your data storytelling. Use these sections for self-reflection, to try to keep your data storytelling as unbiased as possible.

ETHICAL CONSIDERATIONS OF DATA STORYTELLING

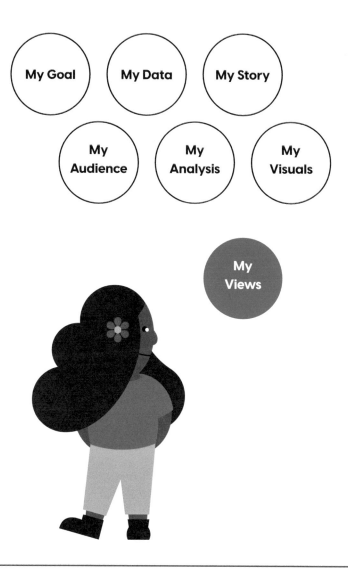

Business stories are told using data storytelling.

Data storytelling is the process of communicating data insights, making it easier for decision-makers (and anyone else) to understand and use the information. Over the next few chapters, you'll gain the knowledge and confidence necessary to navigate the data storytelling process.

WHEN ASKED TO "MAKE YOUR DATA TELL A STORY," YOUR FIRST QUESTION SHOULD ALWAYS BE "WHY?"

DATA STORYTELLING PROCESS

Why: The Business

Why do you want to communicate?

Who: The Audience

Whom will you communicate with?

What: The Data Story

What is your message?

How: The Telling

How will you communicate your data story?

CHAPTER 3

The Business

How data storytelling
creates business impact

The first step in the data storytelling process is to understand your need to communicate.

This book focuses on data storytelling to improve business data communication—hence this chapter's name. However, there are other fields to which data storytelling would also add value (for example, in <u>government</u>, <u>science</u>, or <u>academic</u> data communication).

Although this chapter specifically refers to business, it's about understanding the world your data story will exist in and its reason to exist. So, if you're using data storytelling outside of a business context, the frameworks covered in this chapter are still relevant—just swap out the business world for your community or field.

Before focusing too much on the data, understand these things about the business:

- **The business problem.** What is the business struggling with? For example, *"We're losing customers"*.

- **The desired goal.** What outcome would minimise the problem? *"We need to improve our customer loyalty"*.

- **The action taken.** What could/did the business do to achieve the goal? *"We contacted our customers with a targeted retention campaign"*.

- **The business impact.** What business value did the action create? *"We saw improved customer retention, which led to an increase in their overall customer lifetime value"*.

YOUR ROAD TO CREATING BUSINESS VALUE

Discover the problem

What is the business struggling with?

Define the goal

What outcome would minimise the problem?

Act

What could/did the business do to achieve the goal?

Determine the impact

What business value could/did the action create?

Discover the Problem

Here are ways to uncover a business problem:

- **Listen to stakeholders.** Talk to employees, suppliers, and customers (or analyse their feedback) to understand their concerns. Stakeholders will often know where a business's pain points are.

- **Analyse performance metrics.** Review key performance indicators (KPIs) to spot trends that could be areas of concern. Identify any significant differences from targets or industry benchmarks.

- **Benchmark against competitors.** Compare your business's performance against competitors to understand where you might be falling short.

- **Understand industry trends.** Stay informed about the latest developments in your industry to anticipate potential challenges.

Tui is a Business Performance Analyst at a large hotel chain.

They gathered guest feedback from various sources, including online reviews, post-stay surveys, and social media comments. Tui used sentiment analysis to understand the common issues mentioned by guests.

During their analysis, Tui discovered a large amount of negative feedback relating to a particular hotel, primarily concerning the check-in process. They used operational data to investigate further and found that the hotel was understaffed during peak check-in times, resulting in long wait times for guests.

But Tui didn't know how to improve the check-in process, only what the data was telling them. So, Tui used data storytelling to share this insight with the business to initiate solution design. They used real feedback from frustrated guests to evoke empathy and illustrate the consequences of the issue. Tui trusted that, collaboratively, a solution would be found to improve the guest experience.

Business problems go hand-in-hand with opportunities.

Identifying business problems presents an opportunity to create impactful change. These opportunities become business goals. For example, imagine you're a vegetarian, and your online supermarket recommends a meat special to you. You are going to think they don't understand you very well and might be discouraged from buying from them again. Your pain point (as a customer) is a business problem for the supermarket, and they have an opportunity to understand you better. The resulting goal (or opportunity) for the supermarket could be to create a more personalised shopping experience for their customers.

Define the Goal

A GOAL IS NOT A THING YOU DO. IT'S THE OUTCOME YOU AIM FOR.

Business goals set the direction for business success.

Goals are outcomes a business wants to achieve—for them to be successful. Whatever a business's goals are, their goals set the direction for those who work there. Everyone working for the business is responsible for helping it reach these goals.

Business goals vary across different businesses. A business with customers who pay a monthly subscription might prioritise the goal of retaining them. But a business selling a one-off purchase might focus more on a goal to acquire new customers.

Not all business goals are big or ambitious.

A business will most likely have many goals.

Some goals are far-reaching and inspirational. For example, a business wanting to improve their customers' experience.

Some goals are specific to individuals. For example, a Customer Analyst aiming to understand why some customers have left the business.

These different goals fit into a goal hierarchy, with more general goals at the top and more specific goals at the bottom. Business goals collectively contribute to a larger vision that aligns with the direction in which the business wants to head.

Some goals will enable other goals. For example, if a business understands why their customers leave, they can more actively retain them. If they retain more customers, the business will have more opportunities to increase their overall profit.

BUSINESS GOAL HIERARCHY

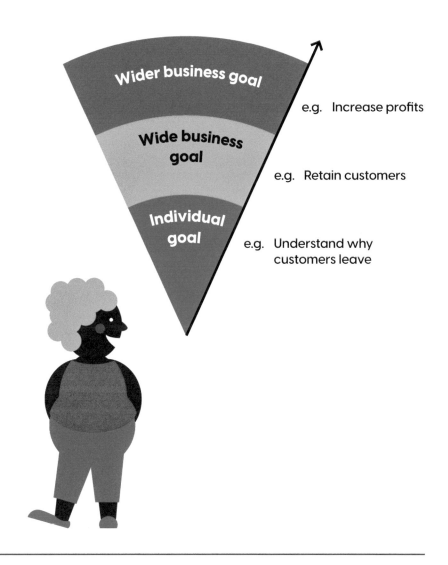

e.g.   Increase profits

e.g.   Retain customers

e.g.   Understand why customers leave

Act

Without action, you won't achieve your business goals.

An action is what specifically needs to happen to achieve a goal. The work of everyone in a business is (hopefully) an action that helps achieve a business goal—even if that action is very small.

Some actions are carried out by teams of people.

Some actions are done by an individual.

A **GOAL** SETS YOUR DIRECTION.

ACTIONS ARE HOW YOU GET THERE.

A goal can be achieved through multiple actions.

A Customer Analyst with the goal of understanding why some customers have left the business could achieve their goal through any of the following actions:

- **Customer Analysis** to find out why they left
- **Competitor Analysis** to see if they have a better offer
- **Customer Survey** to ask them why they left
- **Customer Feedback** to learn what they don't like

When one goal can be achieved through different actions performed by different people, this goal is shared.

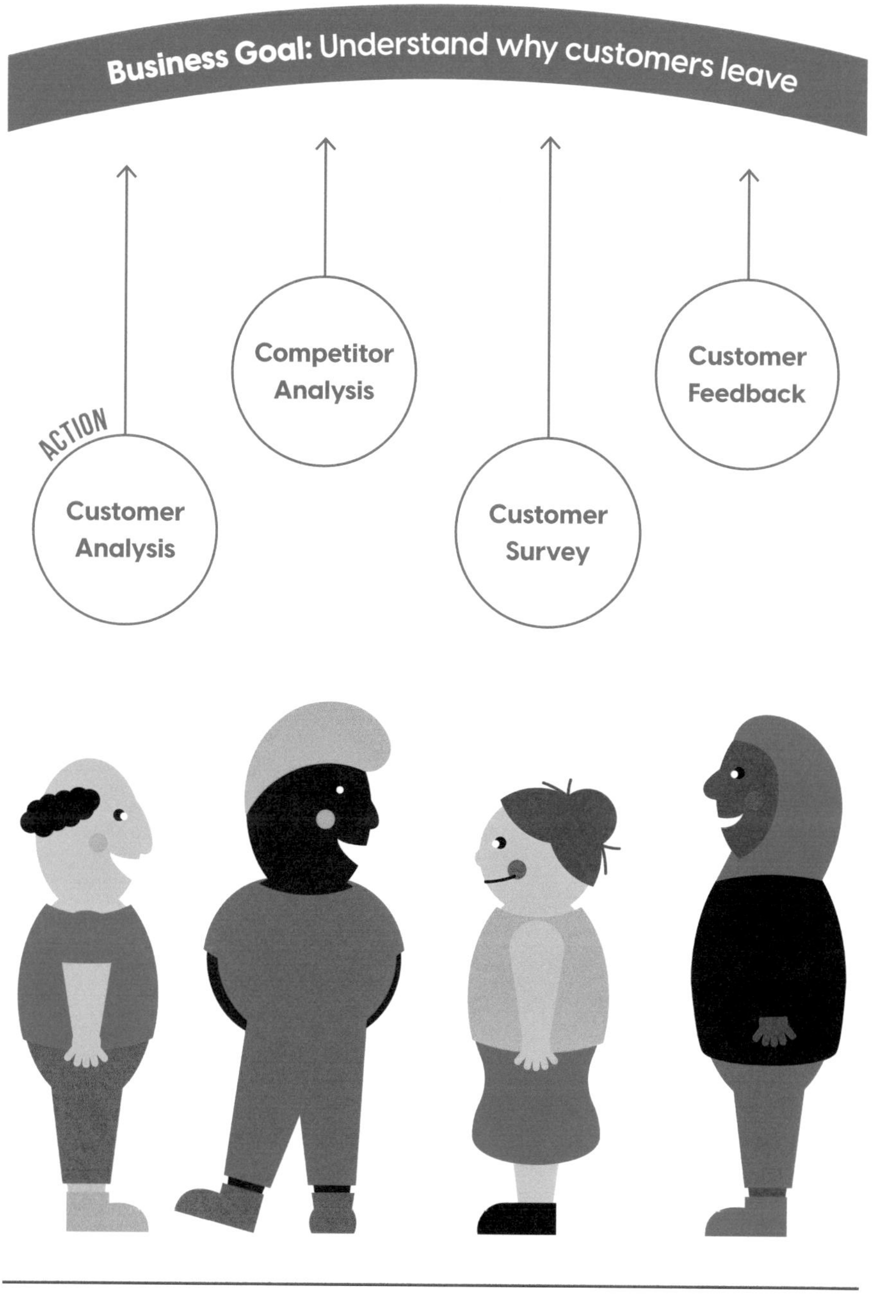

Business Goal: Understand why customers leave

ACTION

Customer Analysis

Competitor Analysis

Customer Survey

Customer Feedback

Actions exist within business goal hierarchies.

Business goals exist in a hierarchy, along with the actions that drive them. A business can have many different and overlapping goal hierarchies.

If you understand what business goal hierarchies your work fits into, it will be easier to communicate the value of what you do. A marketer developing a loyalty program will likely appreciate information from a Customer Analyst on why customers leave the business.

Some business actions don't immediately achieve a goal, but instead support other actions that do. Building a customer churn model won't help retain customers until it's used as part of a retention campaign.

If you understand the goals and actions of other teams (both upstream and downstream in your business goal hierarchy), you'll find it easier to influence and work more collaboratively with them.

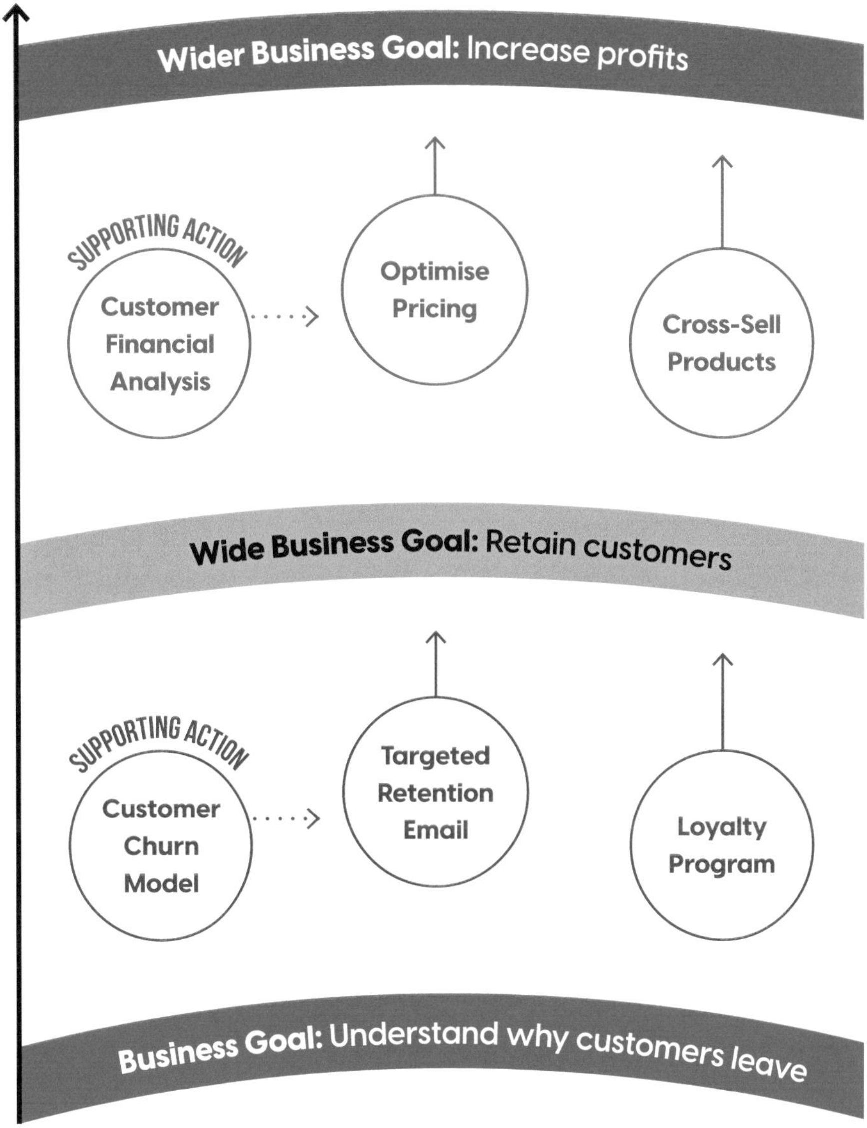

Wider Business Goal: Increase profits

SUPPORTING ACTION

Customer Financial Analysis

Optimise Pricing

Cross-Sell Products

Wide Business Goal: Retain customers

SUPPORTING ACTION

Customer Churn Model

Targeted Retention Email

Loyalty Program

Business Goal: Understand why customers leave

Natalie is the leader of a Business Intelligence team at a large telecommunications company.

Her team of Analysts has recently been established with the goal of helping the business become more data-driven. So, Natalie is on the lookout for ways the team could add value.

She discovered the company's marketing team was preparing an expensive campaign to build customer loyalty. They planned to contact all customers. Natalie knew they could save money by contacting only the customers who were at risk of leaving the business (as predicted by data). But would the marketing team be open to it?

The marketing team had a goal to improve customer retention and a goal to increase profits. The first goal usually drove the second: more customers meant more profits. But this wasn't always the case. If the team spent a large amount of their budget contacting all customers, this might help with retention, but it would cut into business profits.

Natalie's team could help them achieve both goals.

Therefore, after a conversation with marketing about her ideas, she launched a customer churn project with the goal of understanding and measuring a customer's risk of leaving the business. Through data analysis, the Business Intelligence team predicted which customers were more likely to leave in the near future.

Natalie knew this analysis was incredibly valuable, but only if she could convince the marketing team to use the output. Because she understood the goals of the marketing team, it was easy to position her team's analysis. She shared only what was relevant to the marketing team given their goals. Natalie emphasised how targeted marketing could still achieve the team's goal to improve customer retention, but it could also help achieve their goal to increase profits.

Her communication resonated with the marketing team (who were grateful for the help), and Natalie was able to operationalise her team's data analysis. She achieved her goal of enabling a more data-driven business.

Your work should help achieve a business goal.

Many people find aspirational business goals hard to relate to. They struggle to connect what they do in their role (their actions) to these wider goals. This can leave people feeling like their work has no purpose.

If this is you, instead of trying to understand where your work fits in from the top down, discover the business problem you're trying to solve. Business leaders should be able to provide guidance with this.

Understanding your business goals and actions (and those of other teams) will enable you to better communicate, collaborate, and influence within the business.

Determine the Impact

SUCCESSFUL BUSINESS **ACTIONS** CREATE POSITIVE BUSINESS **IMPACT.**

Business impact is the effect an action has on a business's overall success.

This impact can be positive or negative and usually relates to things like financial performance, operational efficiency, customer satisfaction, market positioning, employee engagement, and overall business growth or stability.

Aroha is a Customer Analyst for an international bank. This month, her customer dashboard shows the number of customers leaving the bank has increased. But Aroha doesn't know why. So, she analyses these customers to try to understand why they're leaving. She hopes any insight she uncovers will enable more informed retention strategies.

Problem	Customers leave the business
Goal	Understand why customers leave
Action	Analyse customers
Impact	Better retention strategies enabled by understanding customer churn

The impact of an action is closely linked to the next goal in the business goal hierarchy.

Sanjay is a Marketing Specialist at the same bank. Despite his marketing efforts, he's struggled to retain certain customers. Sanjay is, therefore, relieved when Aroha approaches him with her data insights. He's now confident in designing a retention offer to appeal to these customers. If the offer succeeds, it increases the lifetime value of that customer to the bank.

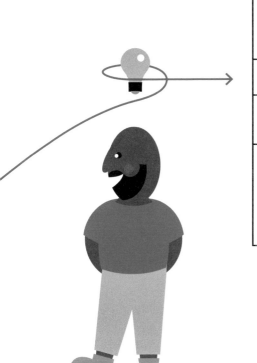

Problem	Certain customers leave the business for specific reasons
Goal	Retain customers
Action	Targeted retention campaign
Impact	Increased life-time value (and potential net profit) through longer customer retention

A **GOAL** IS THE OUTCOME YOU WANT TO CREATE.

IMPACT IS THE VALUE YOU DO CREATE.

Data Stories Revolve around Business Actions

Data storytelling can occur before or after business actions.

A data story can <u>influence</u> business decisions about future actions. This data storytelling happens before the action and helps sell its potential impact. For example, using a data story to create a business case for a marketing campaign.

A data story can <u>share</u> the outcome of past business actions. This data storytelling happens after the action and helps to share the impact and learnings it delivered. For example, using a data story to explain how the above marketing campaign performed.

These two ways are how data storytelling can support business actions.

Discover the problem

What is the business struggling with?

Define the goal

What outcome would minimise the problem?

INFLUENCE

Act

What could/did the business do to achieve the goal?

Determine the impact

What business value could/did the action create?

SHARE

It's rarely as simple as one data story, and then you're done.

There will be times when you need to **share** the impact of one action before you can **influence** another. These two messages (to share and influence) can be delivered as part of the same data story or separately. It might take more than one data story to influence someone to act because it takes multiple data stories for them to know enough to make an informed decision.

There are other times when you'll want to **influence** multiple audiences. When seeking approval for a business case, different stakeholders might require different data communications. You might create a specific data story for your manager, but then a slightly different data story for a C-level executive (based on their unique priorities).

A SUITE OF DATA STORIES

Some audiences need <u>multiple</u> data stories to act.

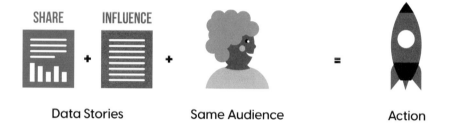

SHARE + INFLUENCE +

Data Stories   Same Audience   Action

Some audiences need <u>different</u> data stories to act.

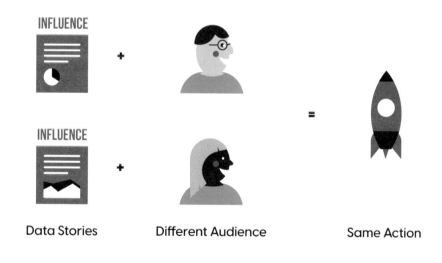

INFLUENCE +

INFLUENCE +

Data Stories   Different Audience   Same Action

DATA STORIES ARE CREATED TO INFLUENCE OR SHARE BUSINESS ACTIONS.

The PGAI Framework

The *Problem-Goal-Action-Impact (PGAI) Framework* defines your business reason to create the data story.

Understanding your specific business **problem**, **goal**, **action**, and **impact** makes explaining how you're contributing to business success much easier.

The next page shows a template for the *PGAI Framework*. Complete this prior to crafting your data story. As will be explained in **Chapter 5: The Data Story**, elements of the *PGAI Framework* can serve as building blocks for your data story.

Tania's *PGAI Framework*

Remember Tania?

You can read her story on page 87.

Problem What is the business struggling with?

The business's website has a low conversion rate (compared to the industry average)

Goal What outcome would minimise the problem?

To increase the website's conversion rate by 25% within three months

---

Action What could/did the business do to achieve the goal?

A/B testing and strategic website changes (this requires additional web development resource)

What are you using data storytelling for?

☺ To influence the action   ☐ To share the action

Impact What business value could/did the action create?

If the goal is met, it will generate $125,000 extra in sales revenue over a three-month period, then more ongoing.

Tui's *PGAI Framework*

Remember Tui?

You can read their story on page 111.

Problem What is the business struggling with?

Over the last six months, the amount of negative guest feedback received by a hotel chain increased.

Goal What outcome would minimise the problem?

The hotel chain understands the guest's reason(s) for providing the negative feedback.

Action What could/did the business do to achieve the goal?

Guest feedback analysed

What are you using data storytelling for?

☐ To influence the action   😊 To share the action

Impact What business value could/did the action create?

The hotel chain makes more informed decisions when designing a solution to improve the guest experience.

Keep It Honest

Ask yourself these questions to help your data storytelling remain as unbiased as possible.

- **What are the broader impacts of my business actions?** A responsible business takes into account the bigger picture of its actions. It's important to understand that data stories, which shape business decisions (and, therefore, actions), can have ripple effects beyond their initial goals. A business action could have unintended social and environmental consequences. By considering all the impacts of your actions, you help your business operate in a way that benefits both people and the planet.

- **Am I trying to persuade (good) or manipulate (bad) my audience?** To answer this question, you need to be aware of your intent. If your communication goal is to influence an action that benefits both yourself and your audience, it's persuasive. But if your goal is to serve a personal agenda and disregard a potentially negative impact on your audience, it's manipulative. Data storytelling should consider the well-being of both parties.

- **Does what I'm trying to achieve align with a business goal?** If it does, this means your actions will not only benefit yourself but also the wider business.

- **Am I being transparent with my stakeholders about my business goals and actions?** Being open about what you want to achieve with your data storytelling means you're less likely to manipulate your audience. It makes your data storytelling more genuine. But it's important to recognise that your audience might not share your motivations, even if their actions appear similar. Different people behave in the same way for various reasons. Understanding the motivations of your audience is discussed more in **Chapter 4: The Audience**.

Understand the business to communicate with impact.

In summary, to communicate or create **impact** with your data storytelling, try to understand what business success looks like. Success is usually a reflection of a business's high-level **goals**.

These high-level **goals** are made up of smaller (more specific) **goals**, which can make them feel more achievable. If you struggle to pinpoint the **goal** of your work, start with the business **problem** you aim to solve.

Business **goals** are achieved through the **actions** of those who work there. **Actions** with positive **impact** drive business success (or the achievement of a business's high-level **goals**).

Data storytelling isn't done to simply entertain an audience with interesting things found in data. A business invests in data storytelling in the hopes that communicating insights to a specific audience has a positive **impact** on the business.

YOU CAN'T TELL A BUSINESS DATA STORY WITHOUT FIRST BEING FAMILIAR WITH THE BUSINESS.

UNDERSTAND YOUR ROAD TO BUSINESS IMPACT.

DATA STORYTELLING PROCESS

Why: The Business

Why do you want to communicate?

Who: The Audience

Whom will you communicate with?

What: The Data Story

What is your message?

How: The Telling

How will you communicate your data story?

CHAPTER 4

The Audience

How to understand whom
you're creating a data story for

Data storytelling is a form of data communication and so, by definition, is created for someone else.

Understanding your audience is vital to creating a data story that will resonate with them. But how to do this in practice is often not well understood. There is more to understanding an audience than simply identifying their job title.

The process of understanding your audience has two parts:

1. Prioritising your audience groups
2. Understanding your priority audience groups

IT'S **EASY** TO DESIGN DATA COMMUNICATION FOR **YOURSELF.** IT'S **HARDER** TO DESIGN IT FOR **OTHER PEOPLE.**

The primary audience for your data story depends on the goal you're trying to achieve.

The *Problem-Goal-Action-Impact (PGAI) Framework* covered in **Chapter 3: The Business** can help you identify the audience based on the outcome you seek from them. For example:

- If you're trying to **influence an action**, who do you want to motivate to act?

- If you're **sharing a previous action**, who do you want to educate so they understand?

Your business goal hierarchy can also help you highlight potential audience groups.

- Who else is trying to achieve your goal?

- Who is responsible for (or impacted by) the actions/goals at levels above yours?

This initial brainstorm will produce a list of different potential groups. You won't necessarily have to communicate with all of these groups, and you'll probably need to present your data story differently across the groups.

Prioritise Your Audience Groups

High Influence

Satisfy	Engage
Try to anticipate and meet their needs	Communicate with regularly and promote joint decisions

Low Interest ← ——————————— → **High Interest**

Update	Inform
Provide essential information only—with minimal effort	Inform and motivate to help deliver the work

Low Influence

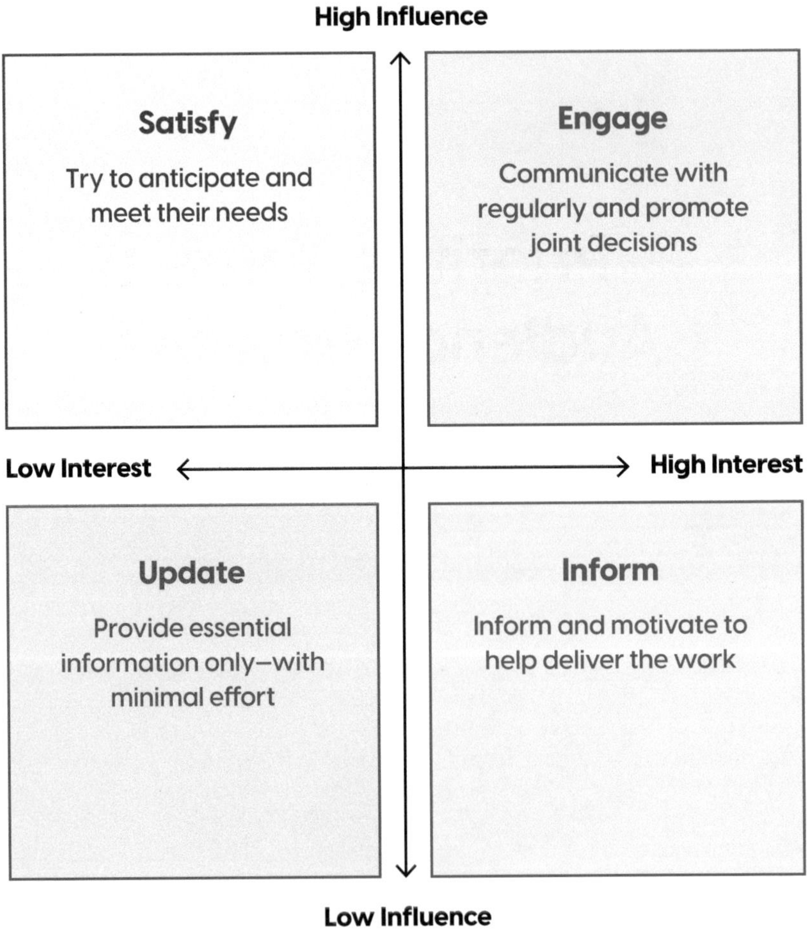

The *Stakeholder Matrix* helps you prioritise your audience groups.

The key groups to focus on are those with high influence. For influential audience groups, focus on their level of interest to determine how you communicate with them. If they're interested, you should be engaging with them often (because they have the power to start or stop the work you do). If they're influential but not interested, they won't need communication as often, but you need to make sure you meet their informational needs.

Audience groups with low influence should also not be ignored. A highly interested audience group has the potential to be a great ally. This group will talk you (and your work) up to others. They might even help you deliver it. They should be kept informed about the work you do—you could even use them as consultants.

You don't need to dedicate a lot of time and resources to groups with little influence who show little interest. However, sometimes, sharing information with this group can increase their interest enough to move them to the right of the matrix, increasing your supporters.

Thabata is an Advisor at a transport agency.

Her job is to offer guidance on how the agency can encourage individuals to use public transport to help achieve climate action goals. But Thabata doesn't want to waste agency resources trying to influence certain people who aren't interested. So, she creates a *Stakeholder Matrix* to determine where the agency should target future communication efforts.

She easily identifies audience groups that need to be highly engaged. These are either people likely to use public transport (commuters and students) or who can influence others to do so (public transport companies). From her matrix, Thabata also understands who her supporters are (parents and environmental groups).

In contrast, the agency will also need to communicate with audience groups who aren't personally interested. For example, elected officials could support policies, funding, and regulatory changes, which promote bus usage for public benefit.

Thabata's *Stakeholder Matrix*

High Influence

Satisfy	**Engage**
Elected officials	Commuters
Urban developers	Students
Other government agencies	Public transport companies

Low Interest ← → **High Interest**

Update	**Inform**
Cyclists	Parents
Taxi services	Environmental groups
Car manufacturers	

Low Influence

You'll need to know more than the name of an audience group to make your data story resonate with them.

Identifying your audience group (or groups) is the first step to understanding them. The importance of different audience groups might change depending on where you are in your project timeline. For example, some audience groups might need a lot of communication at the beginning of a project.

The next step is to develop empathy for your audience groups. Understanding their motivations will help you write a data story that resonates with them. If your *Stakeholder Matrix* highlighted multiple high-priority audience groups, they might need different communications depending on what's important to them.

Understand Your Priority Audience Groups

The more you understand an audience, the more likely you'll be able to create a data story that resonates with them.

Demographics are a common way to try to understand people. For example, segmenting people based on how old they are or how much money they make. Demographics offer easy boxes to put people in. But unless those metrics are relevant to your data story, they're unlikely to help you understand your audience.

To connect a data story with your audience, try to understand their psychographics instead. Psychographics refers to why people do things. This includes people's interests, attitudes, goals, problems, and opinions about your topic.

User Stories help you consider an audience's psychographics.

User Stories are written from the perspective of an end user. They originate from the agile software development process, where they are used as a way to capture user requirements.

User Stories are written using this simple template:

As an [insert audience], **I want...** , **so that**...

For example, a *User Story* written by a Software Developer to help understand their end user describes who the end user is, what the end user wants, and why the end user wants it. This understanding makes it easier for them to design something fit for purpose.

However, when used as part of the data storytelling process this template doesn't solely focus on the end user. It also takes into account the needs of the Data Storyteller. In this case, *User Stories* help not only understand what your audience needs but also how to influence them.

USER STORY

As an: [insert your audience]

I want: [insert what YOU want them to want]

So that: [insert whatever motivates THEM to want what YOU want them to want]

... I want you to want me. I need you to need me.

It sounds like a song by Cheap Trick!

When writing a data story, it's not only about your audience.

As the Data Storyteller, you'll also want something back from them—perhaps to influence someone to act or to help them understand.

User Stories allow you to consider what motivates your audience to act in a certain way, which might differ from your own.

People do things for different reasons. What's important is that they <u>do the thing</u>, not <u>why</u> they do it. For example, some people catch public transport because they care about reducing carbon emissions—while others catch public transport because it saves them money.

Trying to influence an audience to act based on your motivation (rather than theirs) is unlikely to succeed. It's good to share your motivations when communicating, but take the time to understand someone else's motivation for doing what you want them to do.

Troy is a Product Analyst at an electronics retailer.

The company is trying to strengthen its reputation for selling environmentally responsible products. With this in mind, Troy carried out a lifecycle analysis for a recently introduced product.

He knew the analysis was important because what he discovered didn't align with company values. But for his work to create any change, others within the organisation also had to understand the implications of the misaligned values. So, he had to communicate his results to the wider business.

Troy was a great analyst and knew that by using data storytelling (instead of just sharing data), he would be more likely to engage people. He spent time thinking about who was in his audience.

Troy wrote *User Stories* to try to empathise with his audience groups and tailored his data story and visuals to resonate with those groups.

Troy's Marketer Audience *User Story*

As a: marketer

I want: (what Troy wants the marketer to want)

to understand this product's lifecycle analysis

So that: (Marketer's motivation to understand Troy's analysis)

I can identify any reputation risk to our brand

Based on this *User Story*, Troy frames his data story around the context of the company's brand to help engage the marketer with his work.

Writing *User Stories* allows you to practice active empathy.

They'll encourage you to think carefully about whom you're communicating with. This simple act of considering your audience (even briefly) helps you create a more persuasive data story.

A disclaimer: *User Stories* don't always represent an audience.

Just because you've written a *User Story* for your audience, it doesn't mean the *User Story* reflects them. You might have some audiences you know nothing about, so you'll guess. This is okay.

You Are <u>Not</u> Your Audience

A common data storytelling mistake is designing your communication in the same way you'd like to receive it—but you are not your audience.

Chances are, your audience has a different data communication preference. For example, creating a dashboard or a data story for your audience is a high-level difference discussed in **Chapter 1: Why Visualise Your Data?**. But even if you know your audience needs a data story, there are still design decisions to make that take into account how your audience wants to be communicated with.

Before writing a data story, answer these questions about your audience.

- How well do they understand your topic?
- How do they prefer to be communicated with?
- How are they likely to react to your message?
- How interested are they in your information?

The answers to these questions fall on a spectrum. These *Empathy Spectrums* help you map an audience's communication preferences and are detailed over the next few pages.

Empathy Spectrums aren't just about your audience.

As a first step, determine where you think your audience sits on each spectrum and plot that.

Next, ask yourself where you sit on each spectrum.

By plotting where you and your audience fall on these spectrums, it will be easier for you to identify any gaps. If large gaps exist between yourself and your audience, you'll need to design something that is very different from your personal communication preferences.

EMPATHY SPECTRUM 1

How well do they/you understand your topic?

Novice   Them   You   Expert

As the Data Storyteller, you're likely to know more about the topic than your audience (see spectrum above). But if you communicate based on your level of understanding, your audience will struggle to understand the message. So, when writing your data story, begin with what your audience knows—not with what you know.

It's easy to forget there was a time when you didn't know something—or how much of a struggle it was to learn. This is known as the <u>curse of knowledge</u> (and no one is immune). To avoid being hexed, begin by putting yourself in the shoes of someone who has just started at the business—then add in any complexity needed for your audience.

EMPATHY SPECTRUM 2

How do they/you prefer to be communicated with on this topic?

Summary   Them   You   **Detail**

This *Empathy Spectrum* often highlights one of the biggest gaps between the Data Storyteller and their audience. If you like a lot of detail on a topic (maybe you're passionate about it or have spent time analysing it in depth), it's common to want to then share this with your audience. But your audience might prefer a summarised format (see spectrum above).

It can feel uncomfortable to use a communication approach that's different from the one you like, but remember, it's about them, not you.

How are they/you likely to react to your message?

Spontaneous   Them   You   **Thoughtful**

People process a message in two ways: <u>spontaneously</u> and <u>thoughtfully</u>—also referred to as gut and facts, feelings and information, or fast and slow. Spontaneous processing results in a quick, emotional decision that the person probably doesn't even know they're making. Thoughtful processing is highly analytical and results in a more considered decision.

People are more likely to spontaneously process a message if they like how it looks, they like the person delivering it, or they respect others who share that view (as seen by the power of influencers!). A simple example could be someone liking the visuals in a report and then choosing to engage with it further as a result.

People are more likely to thoughtfully process a message if it's relevant to them (and they have the time and head space to think about it). So, if you want someone to make a thoughtful decision, don't ask at 5pm on a Friday!

You'll likely want an audience to process your data story thoughtfully—but often, there are lots of little spontaneous decisions that need to happen first.

If you think your audience will react spontaneously to your data story (see previous spectrum), here are two ways to respond:

1. Lean into their spontaneous reaction. Design your message to emotionally appeal to them in a positive way.

2. Try to provoke a more thoughtful reaction by creating *User Stories* to make your communication more relevant.

3. If possible, meet with people from your audience group beforehand. This helps you gather feedback on your data story and build a rapport with them, increasing their likelihood of making a positive spontaneous decision.

Ideally, design your data stories to appeal to both spontaneous and thoughtful audience reactions.

Salomé operates a digital marketing agency.

She was hired by a family-owned restaurant to run a campaign. The restaurant's owner was reluctant to embrace digital advertising, but was struggling to gain customers through a word-of-mouth approach.

After analysing the campaign's results, Salomé saw that although restaurant foot traffic increased, this didn't translate into sales. She knew this would be a point of concern for the restaurant owner. Salomé considered how to turn what would likely be a spontaneous negative reaction from the restaurant owner into something more positive.

When sharing her results, Salomé showcased the positive online reviews. This way, the restaurant's customers helped deliver her message. She discussed strategies to create repeat customers, thereby boosting sales.

Over time, with Salomé's guidance, the restaurant integrated digital marketing into its marketing strategy.

EMPATHY SPECTRUM 4

How interested are they/you in your information?

Low interest Them You **High interest**

This spectrum was first introduced in the *Stakeholder Matrix* (page 156). If your audience is very interested in your work, they're easier to communicate with. But if they're not as interested as you (see spectrum above), you'll need to encourage them by tailoring your data story to their motivations and communication preferences.

The less interested an audience is, the more persuasive your data story needs to be. Consider their current level of knowledge, along with the amount of detail they prefer to receive on the topic. Make your communication emotionally appealing and relevant to them.

Keep It Honest

Ask yourself these questions to help your data storytelling remain as unbiased as possible.

- **How does someone who is represented in my data feel about the way I'm choosing to communicate it?** When your audience is represented by the data you're sharing, consider how they'll feel. Aligning your data storytelling with their communication preferences builds trust, empathy, and respect—and, in turn, enhances engagement.

- **Does my audience have confirmation biases that might affect how they interpret the data?** Confirmation bias leads people to selectively focus on (and remember) the information that aligns with what they already believe, while ignoring information that contradicts their beliefs. When sharing data, it's important to acknowledge this bias and its influence on how an audience perceives and interprets data.

- **What current events might impact how my audience perceives the information?** Current events shape people's perspectives, emotions, and priorities—potentially influencing how they interpret the data. When communicating your data, acknowledge these influences and explain how the data relates to the current landscape.

- **Do I need to be aware of any potentially sensitive topics for my audience?** When communicating data, be mindful of topics that could trigger emotional responses or cultural concerns. Acknowledge any sensitive subjects up front. This demonstrates respect and cultural awareness and will shape how your audience interprets the information.

- **How do I plan to engage with my audience's questions and concerns to ensure a well-rounded discussion?** Your data story is not the end of the conversation. Engaging with your audience's questions and concerns is essential to build trust and credibility. Addressing their concerns leads to more informed discussions and deeper insights.

Understand your audience to make your data story connect.

In summary, the better you understand an audience, the greater your capacity for empathy towards them. This increases your likelihood of crafting a data story that resonates with them and makes them act in a way that creates business impact.

How you go about trying to understand your audience depends on the amount of access you have to them. For some audience groups, you can simply ask about their preferred communication style. For others, you won't know much about them, so it's okay to research them or make educated assumptions. Just taking time to consider your audience will help develop your empathy for them, even if they are unknown to you.

YOUR AUDIENCE CREATES BUSINESS IMPACT, NOT YOUR DATA STORY.

YOUR DATA STORY IS JUST THE MESSENGER.

DATA STORYTELLING PROCESS

Why: The Business

Why do you want to communicate?

Who: The Audience

Whom will you communicate with?

What: The Data Story

What is your message?

How: The Telling

How will you communicate your data story?

CHAPTER 5

The Data Story

How to find and write a message from data

It's a common misconception that a data story is synonymous with a data visual.

Creating a data story involves combining data insights within a story structure. There are no visuals involved.

However, although a data story is distinct from a data visual, it's usually communicated using data visualisation. This is why the term "data storytelling" is frequently linked to data visualisation. **Chapter 6: The Telling** covers how to use data visuals to tell a data story.

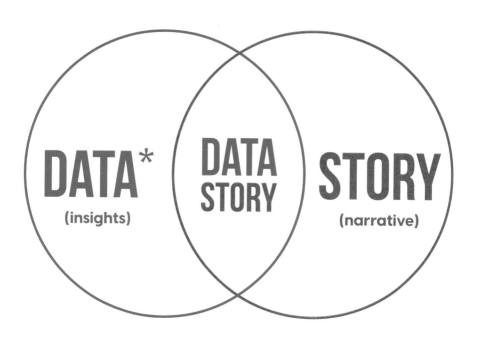

* A DATA STORY IS ACTUALLY CREATED USING DATA INSIGHTS, NOT RAW DATA.

Data analysis can highlight many data insights.

An important and sometimes challenging part of data storytelling is editing. Having a direction when analysing data (for example, starting with a question to answer) helps focus your scope and, therefore, story. But you'll still likely discover many data insights as part of the analytics process.

While these insights might be interesting, it doesn't always mean they're part of the same data story. A common data storytelling mistake is to combine separate data stories and dilute the message.

Effective data storytelling communicates a single story supported by data. It's, therefore, important to determine what data belongs in each story before you begin writing it.

The Data

How to find the building blocks of a data story

All data stories, at a minimum, include a Character, Time, and Data Metric.

A <u>character</u> is whoever (or whatever) the data story is about. Some data stories feature more than one character.

A <u>time</u> is when the data metric is measured. Some data stories compare data measurements at more than one time.

A <u>data metric</u> is what is measured about the character at the time. It's what the story is about.

It's important to identify these key elements before writing your data story.

The Basic Building Blocks of All Data Stories

Your data story character(s) is whoever or whatever your data story is about.

A data story character could be a person (or a group of people), a country, a business, a product, or an animal. Data story characters are not like fictional book characters. You don't need to develop a backstory for your data story character unless that helps you communicate your data.

Characters are a way to introduce contrast into your data storytelling. Comparing characters lets you highlight their differences, helping make any data about them relative and, therefore, more meaningful to the audience.

EXAMPLES OF DATA STORY CHARACTERS

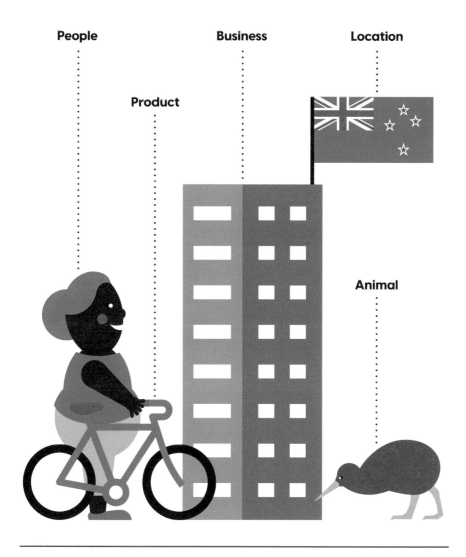

Your data story character is not the same as your audience unless your story is about them.

Your <u>character</u> is whom your data story's <u>about</u>.

Your <u>audience</u> is whom your data story's <u>for</u>.

These may or may not be the same.

For example, a Public Health Advisor analyses the impact of a national outbreak and shares this with their team. The **general public** is the data story **Character** (because the outbreak data is about them), but the **Advisor's team** is the **Audience**. Therefore, the Advisor designs their data storytelling to resonate with their team and not necessarily the general public.

This same data is later shared with the **general public**, who are now both the data story **Character** and **Audience**. So, the Advisor designs their data storytelling to resonate with the general public and not necessarily their team.

Try to identify whom you're designing your data storytelling for without losing sight of whom your data story is about.

THE **CHARACTER** IS WHOM YOUR DATA STORY IS **ABOUT**.

THE **AUDIENCE** IS WHOM YOUR DATA STORY IS **FOR**.

A data metric is what is measured about the character.

Salary is a data metric to describe an employee. Net profit is a data metric to describe a business. Gross domestic product (GDP) is a data metric to describe a country. Height is a data metric to describe a person.

In every data story, there's a main data metric. While other supporting data metrics are likely included in the story, the main data metric is central to the narrative. It holds the most important information and sets the direction of the story.

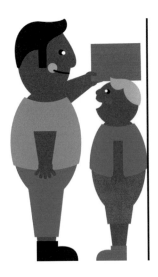

EXAMPLES OF CHARACTER DATA METRICS

Character   Data metrics

Employee

Salary

Wellbeing

Performance

Business

Net Profit

Market Share

Inventory Turnover

Country

GDP

Inflation Rate

Sunshine Hours

A character's data metric has many measurements.

A data measurement is a data metric's value for a character at a specific moment in time. For example, height is a data metric that can be measured multiple times in a person's life.

A data metric can be measured for different characters and at various points in time. Comparing data measurements shows how characters differ from each other or how a character changes over time. This comparison helps an audience better understand the data.

Comparing data measurements is a good way to add contrast to a data story, provided it makes sense to do so.

DATA METRIC TAXONOMY

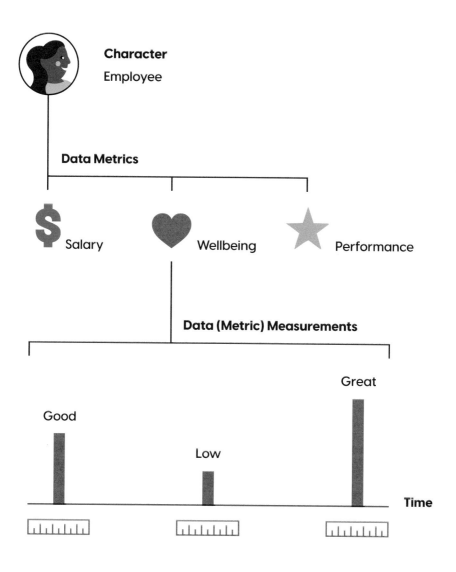

To compare data metric measurements, the character or the time they're measured needs to be the same.

Measurements of the same data metric are easy to compare. They make it possible to analyse a character over time or compare them to other characters.

A management consultancy is a character. The data metric used to assess their performance is net profit. This year, the net profit is $400,000, while last year, it was $200,000. Comparing measurements of this data metric allows an audience to understand its relative change over time.

IS THE SAME DATA METRIC COMPARABLE?

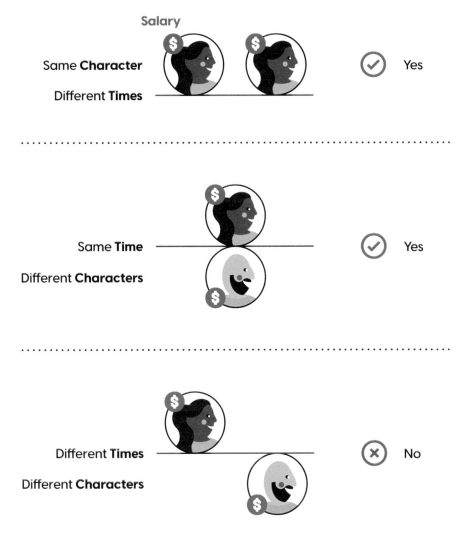

Salary

Same **Character**
Different **Times** — ✓ Yes

Same **Time**
Different **Characters** — ✓ Yes

Different **Times**
Different **Characters** — ✗ No

Be careful when comparing different data metrics.

For different data metrics to be compared, at least the character and time need to be constant. For example, comparing this year's **net profit** with last year's **revenue** doesn't help the audience understand either data metric accurately.

But comparing this year's **net profit** with this year's **revenue** might provide some meaningful insight. Because net profit is calculated using revenue, the data metrics are related and can be compared—but this isn't always the case.

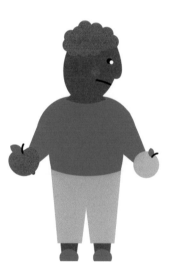

ARE **DIFFERENT** DATA METRICS COMPARABLE?

Salary   Expenses

Same **Character**

Same **Time**

 Sometimes

Same **Character**

Different **Time**

 No

Same **Time**

Different **Characters**

 No

Build a data story around comparable data measurements.

Powerful data stories compare measurements of the same data metric. When creating a data story, there are two ways to contrast the data measurements:

1. <u>Time</u> data contrast. For example, a Finance Manager's current salary compared with their salary last year.

2. <u>Character</u> data contrast. A Finance Manager's current salary compared with an Operations Manager's current salary.

In both approaches, the same data metric is measured (salary), but the data measurements contrast either different times (current vs. last year) or different characters (Finance Manager vs. Operations Manager).

This contrast distinguishes the two main types of data stories: *Time* and *Character*. Each type of data story requires specific building blocks (or pieces of information) to create its narrative.

WAYS TO CONTRAST DATA MEASUREMENTS

Time contrast

Measures the <u>same</u> data metric for the <u>same</u> character at **different moments in time**.

Data measurements

. . . .

Character contrast

Measures the <u>same</u> data metric at the <u>same</u> moment in time for **different data story characters**.

TIME DATA STORIES FOCUS ON A CHARACTER'S CHANGE.

1 YEAR AGO   TODAY

CHARACTER DATA STORIES FOCUS ON CHARACTERS' DIFFERENCES.

TODAY

Gathering information to explain your data insights is an extension of the analytics process.

When you've discovered insight through data analysis, the next step on the road to business impact is to explain it— understand why something happened, what impact it had, and how someone should react to it. Knowing these answers helps shape how you communicate the data insight.

The Building Blocks of Time Data Stories

1 YEAR AGO   **TODAY**

All *Time* data stories have similar building blocks (or specific pieces of information).

Time data stories focus on a character's <u>change</u>. A significant character change usually results in an interesting data story.

At a minimum, *Time* data stories have a character, a data metric, and two time points. These are their most basic building blocks, and together, they describe a character's change, but more blocks help create a more comprehensive narrative.

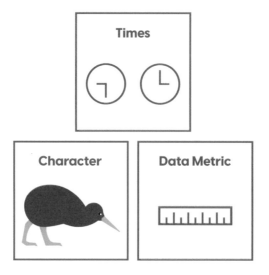

Gather your building blocks before writing your data story.

The *Time Data Story Canvas* (as seen on the next page) helps organise your building blocks. It can be split into two parts.

The first part of the canvas defines your character's change. When arranged together, the basic building blocks help you explain how your character has changed in reference to a data metric.

The second part of the canvas helps you understand and explain the significance of the character's change. This includes building blocks that might require more time and effort to answer.

Each building block is further detailed over the next few pages (pages 214 to 230). See page 232 for a completed *Time Data Story Canvas*.

TIME DATA STORY CANVAS

1. Data Metric What **Data Metric** is changing?

2. Character Whom (or what) does the **Data Metric** describe?

3. Times

Select two time points when the **Data Metric** will be measured (to highlight its change).

Time 1	Time 2

4. Data Change

Record the **Data Metric**'s measurements at **Times** 1 and 2.

Calculate the difference between data measurements (or the **Data Metric**'s change).

Data (Time 1)	Data (Time 2)
Change	

5. Character Change (an expression)

Times + Character + Data Metric + Data Change

6. Impact How was the **Character** impacted by the **Data Change**?

☐ Positively   ☐ No change   ☐ Negatively

7. Reason Why did the **Character Change** happen?

8. Unknowns What don't you know about the **Character Change**?

9. Reaction How do you respond to the **Character Change**?

What was learned from **Reason**?	What can be done to remove **Unknowns**?	What can be done to improve **Impact**?

10. Context What else does your audience need to know to understand the **Character Change**?

Data Metric

What *Data Metric* is changing?

Time data stories use data to show how a character changes over time. The change is measured using a specific data metric. For this type of data story, the data metric is measured twice to contrast the character at different moments in time.

For a business, the following data metrics are some of the many that can change over time:

- Net profit
- Customer acquisition cost
- Production yield
- Employee turnover rate
- Website traffic

Time data story metrics are found using time series data.

Character

Whom (or what) does the *Data Metric* describe?

Here are examples of characters in *Time* data stories:

- If the character is an **animal population**, changing numbers tell a story about species conservation.

- If the character is a **business**, changing customer churn rates tell a story about customer loyalty.

- If the character is a **product**, changing battery life tells a story about product improvement.

In some cases, a changing data metric reflects the change of different characters at the same time. For example, a **customer** leaves a business, and a **business** loses a customer.

If your main character isn't obvious, determine which affected party your audience is most interested in. Are they more concerned with the impact on the business or the impact on the customer? Check out the Impact building block on page 225.

Times

When will the *Data Metric* be measured (to highlight its change)?

Time data stories have two time points, defining the period in which the character's change will be measured. Depending on the data story, time points can be a single moment in time or a timeframe.

Moments in time

- Number of customers **one year ago**
- Number of customers **right now**

Timeframes

- Net profit of the **first year of operation**
- Net profit of the **third year of operation**

The data metric is measured at each time point. These time points can be in the past, present, or future.

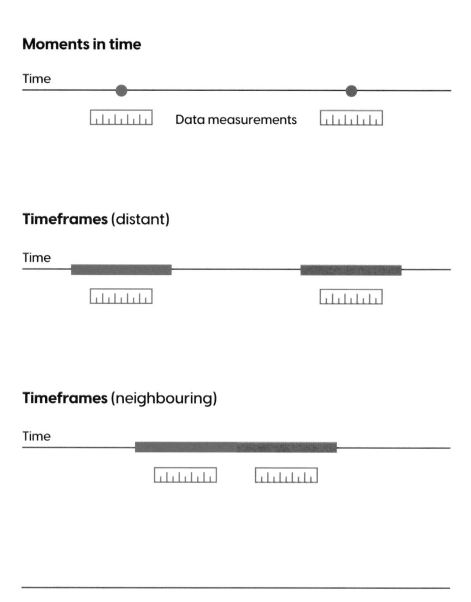

Data Change

[measurements]

How did the *Data Metric* change?

A data metric is measured for each time point. Comparing these measurements shows how the data metric changes over this time.

For example:

Data Metric: Net profit

Times: This year vs. last year

Data Measurement (this year): $3M

Data Measurement (last year): $2M

Data Change: Net profit increased by 50%

A data metric's change is a form of data contrast (something important for data storytelling).

ONE DATA METRIC, TWO DATA MEASUREMENTS

Data Metric: Net profit

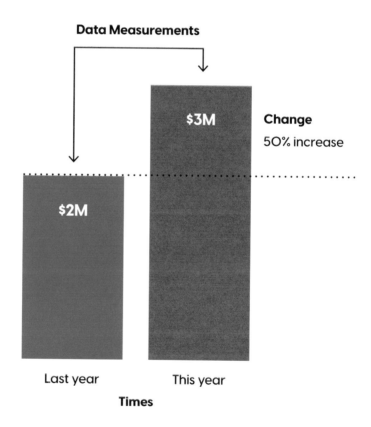

TIME DATA STORY: **BUILDING BLOCK 5**

Character Change

[an expression]

How did the *Character* change?

This building block is a combination of the previous four blocks. Together, these blocks create an expression.

Times + Character + Data Metric + **Data Change**

The expression for the previous net profit example is:

In the last year, the business's net profit **increased by 50%.**

EXAMPLE OF A CHARACTER CHANGE

Data Metric: Life expectancy

Character: People in the Americas

Times: 2019 and 2021

Data Measurement (2019): 76.7 years

Data Measurement (2021): 74.2 years

Data Change: Decreased 2.5 years

. . . .

Character Change:

Between 2019 and 2021, the life expectancy of people in the Americas **decreased by 2.5 years.**

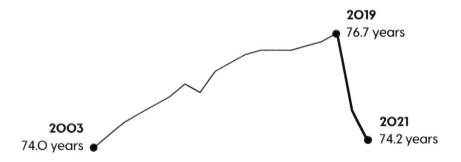

2019
76.7 years

2003
74.0 years

2021
74.2 years

Data: ourworldindata.org

TIME TO **REFLECT**— YOU'VE REACHED THE **CANVAS CHECKPOINT.**

THIS WILL HELP YOU DETERMINE THE IMPORTANCE OF YOUR CHARACTER CHANGE.

An audience won't be interested in all *Character Changes.*

Your data analysis is likely to highlight many character changes, but completing a full canvas for each of these will take you time. Therefore, curating a selection of character changes to focus on is an important part of the data storytelling process. To turn the right ones into data stories, make sure they are suitable for your goal and audience (and not just interesting to you). For example, data analysis uncovers the following character changes:

In the last year, business customer churn **increased by 10%**

In the last week, business web visits **decreased by 20%**

In the last month, business marketing spend **increased by 5%**

In the last year, business net profit **increased by 50%**

If the goal is to understand why customers leave, the first expression would be further developed. But if the goal is to understand what's contributing to business profitability, the last one would be further developed. Both character changes might be related, but each views the story through a different lens (or data metric).

Use the diagram on the next page to help decide if you should continue to develop a character change.

TO DEVELOP OR PARK A CHARACTER CHANGE?

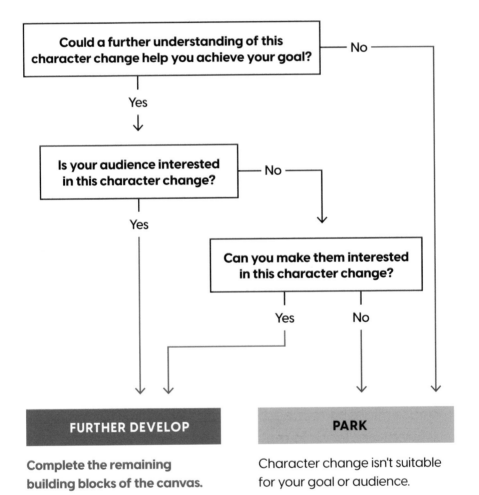

FURTHER DEVELOP

Complete the remaining
building blocks of the canvas.

PARK

Character change isn't suitable
for your goal or audience.

TIME DATA STORY: **BUILDING BLOCK 6**

Impact

How was the *Character* impacted by the *Data Change*?

Understanding how a character is impacted by the change sets the tone of a data story—but it also makes it easier for you to communicate to an audience why they should care.

The impact on a character can be positive, negative, neutral (nothing), or a mix of these. When a character isn't impacted, the data story isn't usually very interesting.

Sometimes, you won't know how a character is impacted by the change because you might not have all the information. This missing building block can become part of your data story. Check out the Unknowns building block on page 228.

To help determine the impact on a business character, understand if a change will prevent or promote the business achieving its goals.

Reason

Why did the *Character Change* happen?

Character changes don't happen without reason. They can be driven by one thing or many. Consider the following character change:

In the last six months, business customer churn increased by 30%.

There were several reasons customers left the business, including declining customer service levels and increased competitor activity. These reasons are also character changes; they just aren't the main focus of this data story. To differentiate a main character change from a reason character change, work out which one drives the other.

Sometimes, the reason for a character change isn't known. In this case, a missing reason can become part of your data story. Check out the Unknowns building block on page 228.

A REASON CAN ALSO BE A CHARACTER CHANGE

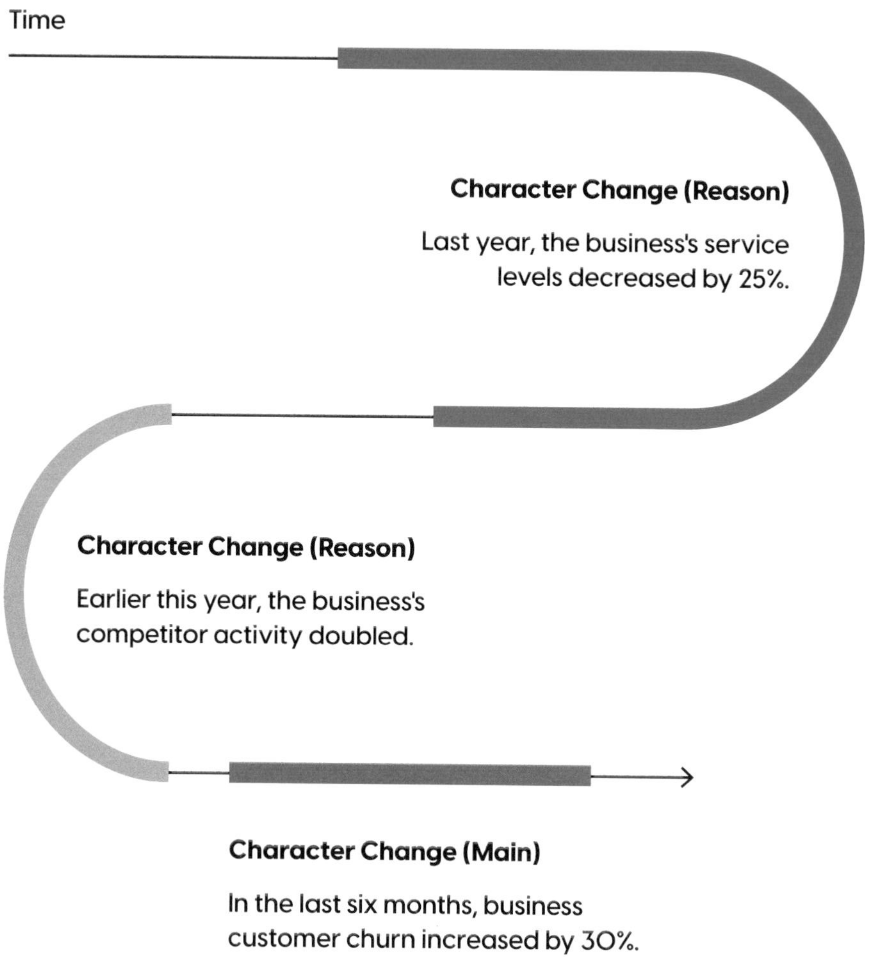

Time

Character Change (Reason)

Last year, the business's service levels decreased by 25%.

Character Change (Reason)

Earlier this year, the business's competitor activity doubled.

Character Change (Main)

In the last six months, business customer churn increased by 30%.

TIME DATA STORY: **BUILDING BLOCK 8**

Unknowns

What don't you know about the *Character Change*?

Use this building block to flag anything about your data metric you're unsure of. You might not know the impact a change has on a character or the reason the change occurred. These missing building blocks can become part of your data story. Understanding what you don't know can help identify future areas of analysis (or next steps).

What's unknown about data is sometimes acknowledged during the analytics process. This could be in the form of missing data or a limitation of the analysis method. Understanding these data unknowns will help you tell a more comprehensive and robust data story.

For example, in New Zealand, some vaccination rates weren't well understood before the National Immunisation Register was established in 2005. Prior to this, the data was collected sporadically through coverage surveys (with sometimes decades between measurements). This limits which time points this data metric can be compared.

Reaction

How can you respond to the *Character Change*?

The previous building blocks (Impact, Reason, and Unknowns) can help determine how you react to a character's change—or how you advise others to. What did you learn from the reason? What can be done to remove any unknowns? What can be done to improve the impact?

Your reaction to a character's change could be to share what you learn for an audience to understand or to influence an audience into taking action. You'll recognise these terms from **Chapter 3: The Business**.

For example, if you have too many things in your Unknowns building block, your data storytelling process might stop here. Or, depending on the audience, your reaction might be to write the data story and highlight the unknowns but recommend further analysis.

Context

What else does your audience need to know to understand the *Character Change*?

Examples of context include explaining to your audience:

- what happened in the past
- the business goal you're trying to achieve
- a technical concept
- why they should care about the character's change

Some audiences need very little context (or background information). Other audiences need a bigger picture. The context needed by your audience depends on their existing knowledge. **Chapter 4: The Audience** looks at ways to help you better understand an audience.

Your data story's context acts as a bridge between your audience's current level of knowledge and what they'll need to know to understand the character's change.

Wei is a freelance Analytics Consultant.

He's been contracted by the marketing team at a leading technology service provider. Their customer churn rate has recently increased, leading to a drop in overall customer numbers. The marketing team needs to better understand the company's falling customer numbers so they can improve their campaign targeting and grow the customer base.

It doesn't take Wei long to understand the data and situation, but he knows the importance of keeping his clients updated throughout the project. So, after his initial analysis, Wei uses data storytelling to help share his findings with the marketing team (and to gauge where he should focus future analysis).

As part of the data storytelling process, Wei completes the *Time Data Story Canvas* to help contextualise his analysis and tell a more balanced data story. You can check out Wei's canvas on the next page.

Wei's *Time* **Data Story Canvas**

1. **Data Metric** What **Data Metric** is changing?	2. **Character** Whom (or what) does the **Data Metric** describe?
Customer numbers	Client's business

3. **Times**	Time 1	Time 2
Select two time points when the **Data Metric** will be measured (to highlight its change).	18 months ago	Today

4. **Data Change**	Data (Time 1)	Data (Time 2)
Record the **Data Metric's** measurements at **Times** 1 and 2.	20,000	15,000
Calculate the difference between data measurements (or the **Data Metric's** change).	**Change** −5,000 (−25%)	

5. **Character Change** (an expression)

Times + Character + Data Metric + Data Change

In the last 18 months, the business's customer numbers have dropped by 25%.

6. Impact How was the **Character** impacted by the **Data Change**?

☐ Positively   ☐ No change   ◎ Negatively

---

7. Reason Why did the **Character Change** happen?

Competitors entered the market at a lower price point, with large activity in specific regions.

---

8. Unknowns What don't you know about the **Character Change**?

What customers left—were they profitable?
Are competitors offering the same services?

---

9. Reaction How do you respond to the **Character Change**?

What was learned from **Reason**?	What can be done to remove **Unknowns**?	What can be done to improve **Impact**?
Some customers are enticed by a competitive offer.	Customer analysis Customer survey Competitor analysis	Target specific regions with competing offers.

---

10. Context What else does your audience need to know to understand the **Character Change**?

Customer churn is a problem for the business.

Like *Time* data stories, *Character* data stories have similar building blocks.

Character data stories focus on the <u>difference</u> between characters. At a minimum, they include two characters, a data metric, and a time point.

The *Character Data Story Canvas* can also be split into two parts. The first part defines the character's difference. The second part helps you understand and explain this difference.

Each building block is further detailed over the next few pages (pages 238 to 246). Some *Character* data story blocks are similar to *Time* data story blocks, and may refer back to this section for more detail. See page 248 for a completed *Character Data Story Canvas*.

The Building Blocks of Character Data Stories

CHARACTER DATA STORY CANVAS

1. **Characters** Whom (or what) are you comparing?	**Main**	**Supporting**

2. **Data Metric** What **Data Metric** are you comparing?	

3. **Time** When will the **Data Metric** be measured?	

4. Data Difference

Record the **Data Metric's** measurements at the **Time**.

Calculate the difference between data measurements.

Difference

5. Character's Difference

Time + Characters + Data Metric + Data Difference

6. Advantage What **Character** is in a better position?

☐ Main character   ☐ No difference   ☐ Supporting character

7. Reason Why are the **Characters** different?

8. Unknowns What don't you know about the **Character's Difference**?

9. Reaction How can you respond to the **Character's Difference**?

What was learned from **Reason**?	What can be done to remove **Unknowns**?	What can be done to improve **Advantage**?

10. Context What else does your audience need to know to understand the **Character's Difference**?

Characters

Whom (or what) are you comparing?

Character data stories have two characters—one <u>main</u> character and one <u>supporting</u>. The main character is the focus of the story. Here are examples of characters in *Character* data stories:

- If the main character is a **kākāpō population** and the supporting character is a **neighbouring island's kākāpō population**, comparing their genetic diversity tells a story about bird species vulnerability.

- If the main character is your **business** and the supporting character is your **competitor**, comparing customer numbers tells a story about market share.

- If the main character is an **iPhone** and the supporting character is a **Samsung phone**, comparing battery life tells a story about product performance.

Data Metric

What *Data Metric* are you comparing?

Character data stories use data to show how characters differ from each other. This difference is measured using a specific data metric.

A business could use the following data metrics to compare the performance of different projects:

- Return on investment
- Actual cost
- Budget variance
- Scope creep
- Risk exposure

CHARACTER DATA STORY: **BUILDING BLOCK 3**

Time

When will the *Data Metric* be measured?

Character data stories have one time point. Like *Time* data stories, time points can be a single moment or a timeframe (see page 216).

For example, **takahē** and **kiwi** bird populations are two different characters. Data metrics to compare them are "current population number" (measured at a single moment) and "population growth" (measured over a timeframe).

Data Difference

[measurements]

What is the difference between data measurements?

The data metric is measured for each character. By comparing measurements, you show how the data metric differs between characters. For example:

Characters: Business (main) and competitor (supporting)

Data Metric: Net profit

Time: This year

Data Measurement (Business): $3M

Data Measurement (Competitor): $4M

Data Difference: The business's net profit was 33% lower

The difference between character data measurements is another form of data contrast.

Character Difference

[an expression]

How is the main *Character* different from the supporting?

This building block is a combination of the previous four blocks (**Time** + **Characters** + **Data Metric** + **Data Difference**). These blocks create an expression.

The character difference for the previous net profit example is: **This year, our business net profit was 33% lower than** our competitor's.

Like *Time* data stories, your audience won't be interested in all the character differences you discover. Some won't help you achieve your goal or be relevant to your audience.

This is the *Character* data story checkpoint. Use the diagram on page 224 to determine if you should complete the remaining building blocks (just replace Character <u>Change</u> with <u>Difference</u>).

EXAMPLE OF CHARACTER DIFFERENCE

Data Metric: Life expectancy

Characters: People in Oceania (main)
People in the Americas (supporting)

Time: 2021

Data Measurement (Oceania): 79.4 years

Data Measurement (Americas): 74.2 years

Data Difference: Oceania was 5.2 years higher

· ·

Character Difference:

In 2021, the life expectancy of the people in Oceania **was 5.2 years higher than that** of the people in the Americas.

Data: ourworldindata.org

CHARACTER DATA STORY: **BUILDING BLOCK 6**

Advantage

What *Character* is in a better position?

The Advantage building block is similar to the Impact building block of *Time* data stories. These blocks are about setting the tone of the story—is the story a positive or negative one?

But unlike *Time* data stories, character differences won't always directly impact each other. So, it's more helpful to understand how the characters are positioned in relation to each other or who has the advantage.

CHARACTER DATA STORY: **BUILDING BLOCK 7**

Reason

Why are the *Characters* different?

Character differences might have always been there, or they might exist because one (or both) characters change. Consider the previous character difference:

This year, our business net profit was 33% lower than our competitor's.

There are several reasons for this difference in net profit, including higher supplier costs, increased customer churn rate, and a more comprehensive service offering by the business's competitor.

Sometimes, the reason for the difference isn't known. In this case, a missing reason can become part of your data story. Check out the Unknowns building block on the next page.

The following building blocks are the same for both *Character* and *Time* data stories. For more detail, see pages 228-230 (just replace the word <u>Change</u> with <u>Difference</u>).

CHARACTER DATA STORY: **BUILDING BLOCK 8**

Unknowns

What don't you know about the *Character's Difference*?

CHARACTER DATA STORY: **BUILDING BLOCK 9**

Reaction

How can you respond to the *Character's Difference*?

CHARACTER DATA STORY: **BUILDING BLOCK 10**

Context

What else does your audience need to know to understand the *Character's Difference*?

How Tania finds her building blocks

Remember Tania?

You can read her story on page 87.

Tania uses the *Character Data Story Canvas* to organise her analysis of website conversion. She's looked at why her company's rate is below the industry average. The canvas building blocks enable her to take a more holistic approach to understanding the low conversion rate and what she could do to improve it.

Check out Tania's *Data Story Canvas* on the next page.

Tania's *Character* *Data Story Canvas*

1. **Characters** Whom (or what) are you comparing? Clothing retailers	**Main**	**Supporting**
	Our business	Others in industry

2. **Data Metric** What **Data Metric** are you comparing?	Website conversion rate

3. **Time** When will the **Data Metric** be measured?	Today

4. **Data Difference** Record the **Data Metric's** measurements at the **Time**.	0.5%	0.8%
Calculate the difference between data measurements.	**Difference** −0.3 pp	

5. Character's Difference

Time + Characters + Data Metric + Data Difference

Today, our website conversion rate is 0.3 percentage points lower than our industry's average.

---

6. Advantage What **Character** is in a better position?

☐ Main character ☐ No difference 🌀 Supporting character

---

7. Reason Why are the **Characters** different?

Our website is cluttered (due to various one-off changes) and isn't optimised for an overall user-friendly experience.

---

8. Unknowns What don't you know about the **Character's Difference**?

We don't know exactly what needs to be changed on the website to improve its conversion rate.

---

9. Reaction How can you respond to the **Character's Difference**?

What was learned from **Reason**?	What can be done to remove **Unknowns**?	What can be done to improve **Advantage**?
Future one-off changes need to be more strategic	A/B testing	Website changes

---

10. Context What else does your audience need to know to understand the **Character's Difference**?

Digital sales account for 25% of total sales ($2m a year). Our website was last optimised for conversion 5 years ago.

One canvas sets the scope of one data story.

A completed *Data Story Canvas* (either *Time* or *Character*) contains the information to write a high-level data story. If you find you want to include information that doesn't fit the canvas, you're likely trying to tell two different data stories. In practice, multiple canvases are often completed in parallel because data analysis usually uncovers more than one data story.

The Story

How to arrange your data insights into a story

You need to understand "story" before "data story".

Stories have held a central role throughout human evolution. They help pass down knowledge and emotions from one generation to another, ensuring valuable insights and experiences are remembered.

But you aren't alone if you're unsure about exactly how to use data to tell a story. Although it seems like something that should come naturally, it doesn't for most people. Much of the struggle stems from not understanding what the term "story" means (in the context of data storytelling).

Therefore, let's start there: how to write a story <u>without</u> data.

How to Write
a ~~Data~~ Story

A story communicates a message.

The practice of writing a story is actually one of clarifying a message for a specific audience. If you understand your message, it will be easier to communicate through a story.

In business, "story" refers to how the information you want to communicate is arranged—or the structure of your narrative.

There's a universal story structure.

Many stories follow the three-act structure. This story structure isn't new. It dates back centuries to Aristotle.

Act 1 (agreement)

Act 1 sets the scene. The main character is introduced, along with any necessary story context. For example, **"Africa's animal kingdom is ruled by lions, and Simba is a young lion who will succeed his father (Mufasa) as king."**

Act 2 (contrast)

Act 2 provides the tension. It causes the narrative to change direction in some way. For example, **"But when Simba's uncle Scar murders Mufasa, Simba is tricked into thinking he is responsible and flees his homeland."**

Act 3 (consequence)

Act 3 explains the consequence of what happened in Act 2, and the story comes to a close with a resolution. For example, **"Therefore, Simba needs to overcome his guilt before he can take his rightful place as king."**

An easy way to understand the three-act structure is the And-But-Therefore (ABT) Framework.

The *ABT Framework* is the brainchild of Science Communicator, Randy Olson. These three words (and their synonyms) advance a story through its three acts.

And is a common agreement word used to join together statements to help set the scene in **Act 1**. Other agreement words include **also, equally, additionally**, etc.

But is a strong contrast word used to introduce **Act 2**. Other contrast words include **however, despite, yet**, etc.

Therefore is a consequence word and introduces **Act 3** to help resolve the story. Other consequence words/statements include **so, as a result, for this reason**, etc.

The *ABT Framework* has been called the "DNA of story" because of its simple structure and how it can be applied to many forms of communication—including data storytelling. The Lion King story example on the previous page follows the *ABT Framework*.

Randy Olson: Houston, We Have a Narrative

EXAMPLES OF THE ABT FRAMEWORK

Hey, I just met you, AND this is crazy.
BUT here's my number, SO call me, maybe.

—Carly Rae Jepsen

Many businesses prioritise data-related activities, such as collection, storage, access control, preparation, modelling, analysis, and visualisation. AND collectively, these activities serve as a fundamental foundation to make well-informed decisions based on data. BUT the value of this backend effort is unrealised until the data insights are used to create business impact. THEREFORE, data insights must be understood beyond the data team. Data storytelling has the power to transform data insights into tangible business value by effectively communicating the meaning and implications of the data.

—Kat Greenbrook (this is my data storytelling elevator pitch)

Many stories in this book use the *ABT Framework*. Can you recognise it?

Structuring your message into three acts makes it more concise and compelling to your audience.

Act 1 can have more than one statement, but they all need to be in agreement with each other. For example, they could all be negative, or they could all be positive. They could all be about one character. They could all be about one period of time. These statements are all setting one scene.

Whatever type of scene is set in **Act 1**, **Act 2** is there to contrast it. For example, if **Act 1** is positive, then **Act 2** could be negative (or even overly positive) and vice versa. This contrast between **Act 1** and **Act 2** helps move the story forward by changing the direction of the narrative. **Act 3** then resolves this conflict.

Because the words BUT and THEREFORE introduce **Act 2** and **Act 3** respectively, they (along with their synonyms) are used only once per story—unlike the word AND, which is there to group together the statements that make up **Act 1**.

How to Write
a <u>Data</u> Story

A data story uses the same three-act narrative structure.

The narrative structure of a story with data is the same as that of a story without data. The difference is a data story communicates a data-derived message.

The *Data Story Canvas* helps gather the building blocks you'll need to write your data story.

A DATA STORY IS A NARRATIVE THAT COMMUNICATES A DATA-DERIVED MESSAGE.

Using the *ABT Framework*, arrange the *Data Story Canvas* building blocks into three acts.

There is no right or wrong way to arrange these building blocks. This is what it means to "craft" a story.

The following are potential ways to arrange the *Data Story Canvas* building blocks into a three-act structure using the *ABT Framework*.

Time data story building block arrangement

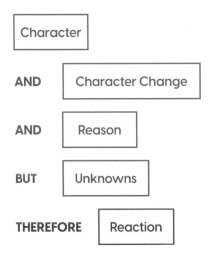

Character

AND   Character Change

AND   Reason

BUT   Unknowns

THEREFORE   Reaction

Time data story alternative building block arrangement

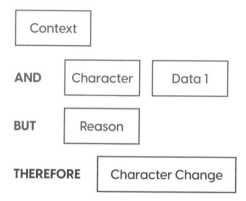

Character data story building block arrangement

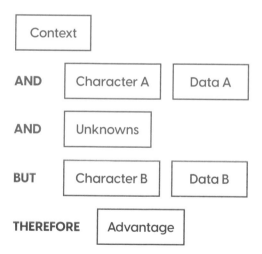

The *PGAI Framework* has more building blocks.

The *PGAI Framework* (covered in **Chapter 3: The Business**) identifies the goal and impact of a specific business action. A data story helps to share or influence this action.

Combining information from the *Data Story Canvas* with the *PGAI Framework* creates more persuasive and strategic communication. The following examples show how building blocks from the *Data Story Canvas* and *PGAI Framework* can be arranged into a three-act structure using the *ABT Framework*. Now, that was a mouthful!

Time data story building block arrangement

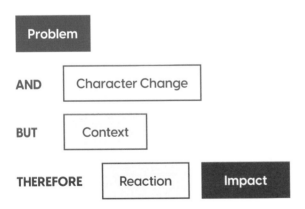

The solid blocks are from the *PGAI Framework*. The rest are from the *Data Story Canvas*.

Character data story building block arrangement

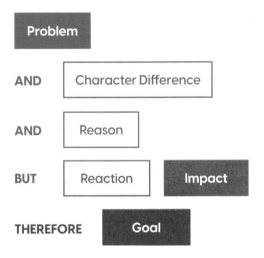

Some building block arrangements might sound stronger or be more suited to a particular audience. Generally, the further removed an audience is from the data or topic, the more context they'll need to understand the data.

The following pages show specific examples of building block arrangements next to their written data story.

How Tania explains her work to the business

Let's revisit Tania. As a way to lift business acumen, she wants to share her work with those outside her team. This audience does not have specialised website knowledge, so Tania knows she has to communicate at a high level (not too much data and not too much jargon).

Using her *Data Story Canvas* (page 248) and *PGAI Framework* (page 143), Tania created a data story to share her work.

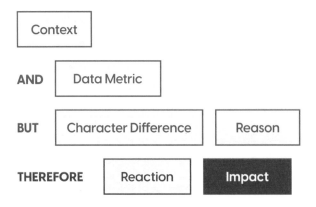

Website sales are an important revenue stream for our business, AND conversion rate measures how well our website converts traffic into online sales.

BUT, when compared to our competitors, our website conversion rate is well below average because our website is cluttered and not optimised for a user-friendly experience.

THEREFORE, I'm currently testing various website changes to identify those that will improve our conversion rate. This work is a great opportunity to boost website sales revenue and enhance the overall buying experience for our customers.

How Tania influences her manager

Tania wrote a different data story to influence her manager for the extra budget. Her manager needs more data detail than a general business audience, but less context. Tania positions her work in terms of how it will contribute to the wider business goals of her manager.

She uses her same *Data Story Canvas* along with her project's *PGAI Framework* to create a data story to influence her manager.

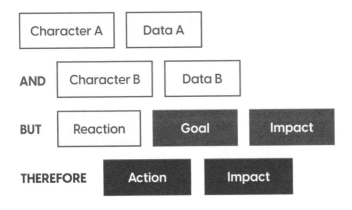

Our current website conversion rate of 0.5% falls below the industry average of 0.8%.

BUT, with A/B testing and strategic website changes, my goal is to increase our conversion rate by 25% (to 0.625%) in three months. This will generate an additional $125,000 in sales revenue.

THEREFORE, to achieve this goal, I need additional web development support. I'm confident the potential for incremental sales revenue justifies this investment, as the improved conversion rate will generate consistent financial benefits beyond the initial three months.

Not all data stories use all building blocks.

The *Data Story Canvas* is a guide to understanding what information you need to tell a balanced data story. It will help you reflect on the data metric you want to explain.

The *PGAI Framework* is a guide to understanding how your data story fits into a business context. It will help you reflect on the impact you're attempting to create.

But your data story doesn't need to include all the building blocks collected in the above canvas and framework. What you include in your data story depends on your audience and the amount of detail you want to share.

How to Add Detail
to a <u>Data</u> Story

CAUTION: HARD STUFF AHEAD. APPROACH WITH A HOT BEVERAGE OF YOUR CHOICE.

A *summary* data story sets the scope of a more detailed narrative. Always start general before getting specific.

In the previous section, the data stories you learned to write were at a summary level. For the majority of data stories you communicate, this might be all you need. *Summary* data stories have only one **but** and one **therefore** (because these words introduce Acts 2 and 3, respectively).

However, when an audience needs more detail, you'll have to expand your *summary* story. A word of warning: this isn't an opportunity to add all that leftover data! The process of fleshing out a data story is a very deliberate one.

SUMMARY DATA STORY STRUCTURE

Summary Act 1

———————————
AND ———————————

Summary Act 2

BUT ———————————
———————————

Summary Act 3

THEREFORE ———————
———————————

The same three-act structure used to create the *summary* data story is used to add the detail.

To create a more detailed version of a *summary* data story, add another data story—but not just any data story!

These additional data stories are known as *nested* data stories (or data stories within data stories). *Nested* data stories provide detail to a *summary* data story. They will always support the *summary* data story and not introduce contrasting information. Each story act (or ABT statement) in a *summary* data story sets the scope for any *nested* data stories within it.

When creating *nested* data stories, keep in mind the hierarchy of your story structure.

DETAILED DATA STORY STRUCTURE

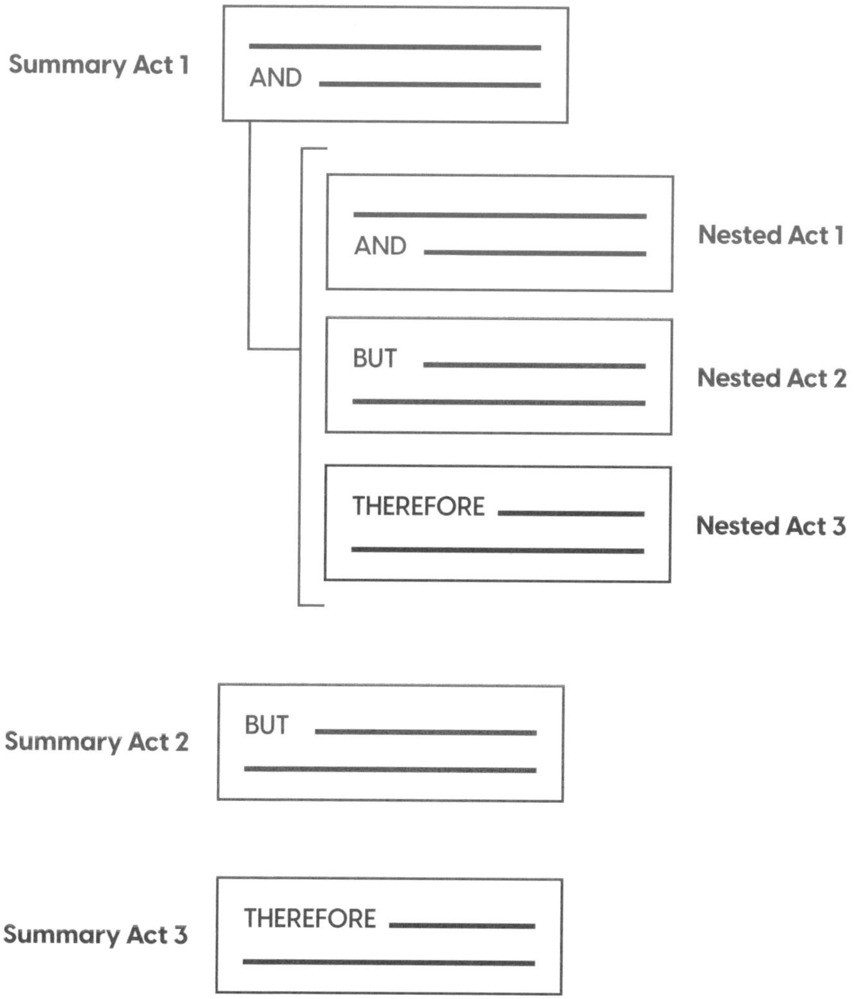

Summary Act 1

AND _____

Nested Act 1

AND _____

Nested Act 2

BUT _____

Nested Act 3

THEREFORE _____

Summary Act 2

BUT _____

Summary Act 3

THEREFORE _____

Add story detail only when it's necessary.

It's important to understand your *summary* data story before going deeper into any detail. This keeps you focused on the overall message and not distracted by those shiny details.

Depending on the detail required by an audience (**Chapter 4: The Audience** has more on this), a *summary* data story can have many *nested* stories. These *nested* data stories aren't always dependent on the *summary* data story they are nested in to be understood. This means that a *nested* data story can stand alone due to its three-act structure (if the audience has enough context).

Nested data stories are helpful if you have different audiences requiring different details about the same *summary* data story.

One data story structure. Two data story types.

Remember the two data story types, *Time* and *Character*?

Data stories (whether they be *summary* or *nested*) have a common three-act <u>structure</u>. But *summary* and *nested* data stories can be different data story <u>types</u>.

For example, a *summary Character* data story (about a character's difference) could use a *Time* data story (about a character's change) to provide more detail. This concept is first explained with a diagram on the next page and then by expanding Tania's *summary* story over the next few pages.

DIFFERENT DATA STORY TYPES

Summary data story (*Character* type)

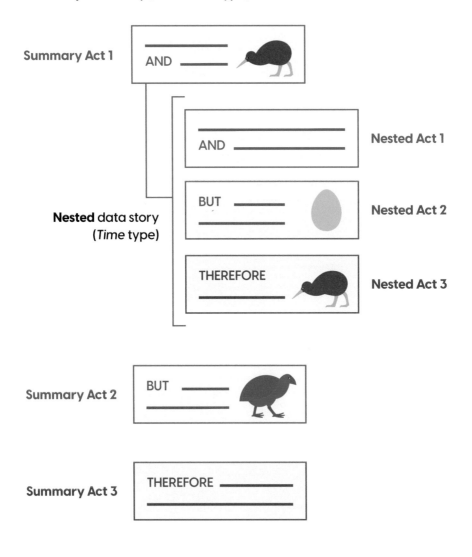

Summary Act 1

Nested Act 1

Nested Act 2

Nested data story
(*Time* type)

Nested Act 3

Summary Act 2

Summary Act 3

How Tania adds detail to her data story

Tania wants to add detail to her *summary* data story on page 267. She specifically wants to expand the following Act 1 statement:

Website sales are an important revenue stream for our business.

Tania knows website sales revenue increased in the last year. Explaining this growth to her audience might demonstrate how important this channel is (and help support the above statement).

Using website sales revenue as her nested data metric, Tania uses a *Data Story Canvas* to gather her building blocks. This *nested* data story is about how the metric changes over time, so she completes the *Time* version of the *Data Story Canvas*.

You can see Tania's *Data Story Canvas* on the next page.

Tania's *Time Data Story Canvas* (*nested*)

1. Data Metric What **Data Metric** is changing? Website sales revenue	**2. Character** Whom (or what) does the **Data Metric** describe? Our business

3. Times Select two time points when the **Data Metric** will be measured (to highlight its change).	**Time 1** 13 – 24 months ago	**Time 2** 1 – 12 months ago

4. Data Change Record the **Data Metric's** measurements at **Times** 1 and 2.	**Data** (Time 1) $1 million	**Data** (Time 2) $2 million
Calculate the difference between data measurements (or the **Data Metric's** change).	**Change**	+ $1 million

5. Character Change (an expression)

Times + Character + Data Metric + Data Change

In the last year, our website sales revenue doubled to $2m.

6. Impact How was the **Character** impacted by the **Data Change**?

☉ Positively ☐ No change ☐ Negatively

7. Reason Why did the **Character Change** happen?

Increased social media presence and marketing activity have driven more traffic to the website.

8. Unknowns What don't you know about the **Character Change**?

Are certain products or customers responsible for driving web revenue?

9. Reaction How do you respond to the **Character Change**?

What was learned from **Reason**?	What can be done to remove **Unknowns**?	What can be done to improve **Impact**?
Activity on socials increases website sales revenue.	Website sales and customer analysis	Improve website conversion rate

10. Context What else does your audience need to know to understand the **Character Change**?

Today, our website accounts for 25% of total sales.

Tania writes another data story using her *Time Data Story Canvas* on the previous page. She makes sure this *nested* data story supports her *summary* story statement. Nothing about her *nested* data story contrasts with her *summary* data story; it just adds more detail to help explain it.

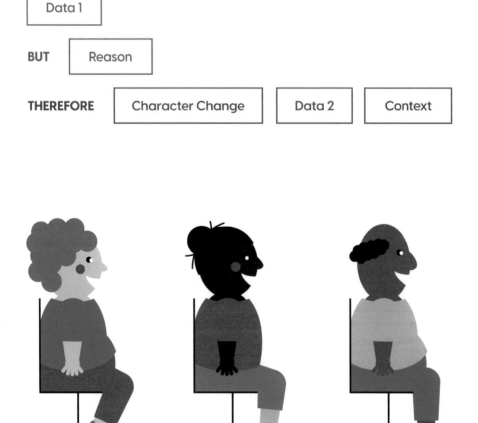

Website sales are an important revenue stream for our business.

Last year, our website sales generated $1 million in revenue.

HOWEVER, this year, we increased our social media presence and marketing activity to drive more traffic to the website and boost our website sales.

SO, due to these efforts, our website sales revenue doubled. Website sales now generate $2 million a year and account for 25% of total sales revenue.

The *nested* data story makes sense even if read without the *summary* story.

Here is the combined (*summary* and *nested*) data story Tania presents to the business:

Summary Act 1   Website sales are an important revenue stream for our business.

Nested Act 1   Last year, our website sales generated $1 million in revenue.

Nested Act 2   HOWEVER, this year, we increased our social media presence and marketing activity to drive more traffic to the website and boost our website sales.

Nested Act 3   SO, due to these efforts, our website sales revenue doubled. Website sales now generate $2 million a year and account for 25% of total sales revenue.

Summary Act 1 (continued...)   Conversion rate measures how well our website converts traffic into online sales.

Summary Act 2   BUT, when compared to our competitors, our website conversion rate is well below average because our website is cluttered and not optimised for a user-friendly experience.

Summary Act 3   THEREFORE, I'm currently testing various website changes to identify those that will improve our conversion rate. This work is a great opportunity to boost website sales revenue and enhance the overall buying experience for our customers.

The *summary* data story still makes sense with the details of the *nested* story.

The best way to build your data story muscle is to practice using it... so, go write some data stories!

Now that you're aware of the three-act structure (and can recognise it through the words **and, but, therefore**, and their synonyms), you'll start to see/hear it everywhere. Journalists often frame their stories around the three-act structure, so watch some news bulletins to witness it in action.

The more familiar you get with this story structure, the more your narrative intuition will develop, making it easier for you to write (and therefore, tell) your data stories.

Chapter 7: The Practice shows the process of writing a detailed data story, with some next steps to practice and build your data storytelling skills.

Keep It Honest

Ask yourself these questions to help your data storytelling remain as unbiased as possible.

- **What is the source of my data? Is it reputable?**
  Understand where your information comes from, the methods used to collect it, and the trustworthiness of the organisation or entity providing it. Assessing your data sources helps you avoid spreading misinformation.

- **Are there any conflicts of interest that might influence how I interpret or present the data?** It's important to address conflicts of interest in data storytelling. These arise from financial or personal ties that might bias your judgment or funding sources that influence how the data is interpreted and communicated. Failing to address these issues could undermine trust in your data.

- **Are there limitations in the methods used to collect and analyse the data?** The reliability of data insight is influenced by limitations in data collection and analysis—such as inadequate sample sizes (a survey might not accurately reflect an entire population), data quality, privacy, and current technological capabilities. It's important to identify these method limitations to ensure a representative data story.

- **Is my narrative a good representation of my data?** Data storytelling requires a rigorous and transparent approach to both data analysis and communication. It involves not only accurately representing your data insights but also providing the context and ethical consideration to ensure its impact and integrity.

- **What's the counter data story—is this also true?** Data can tell different stories based on the context in which it's examined. For example, a number can appear low or high depending on what it's compared to. This highlights the subjectivity of data interpretation. By considering the counter-data story, you take a more critical and open-minded approach to data analysis. You recognise that multiple (true) stories can be found in the same dataset.

- **What assumptions have I made? Do I understand why I've made them?** You will likely make assumptions as part of the data storytelling process. These include things like how accurate the data is, causation vs. correlation, audience knowledge, stakeholder interests, as well as how influenced you are by your own biases. If these assumptions are incorrect, they can influence the credibility of your data story. Data storytelling assumptions are okay to make as long as you can sensibly justify why you've made them.

Data stories are structured arrangements of information building blocks.

Your data story's building blocks are driven by a specific data metric. The challenge is to find a data metric with measurements different enough to hold someone's attention because not all data stories are interesting.

When you've gathered these building blocks, using the three-act structure to arrange them into a data story is relatively straightforward. However, it's only when you're clear on what your data story is that you're ready to tell it.

WRITE DOWN YOUR DATA STORY BEFORE TRYING TO TELL IT.

DATA STORYTELLING PROCESS

Why: The Business

Why do you want to communicate?

Who: The Audience

Whom will you communicate with?

What: The Data Story

What is your message?

How: The Telling

How will you communicate your data story?

CHAPTER 6

The Telling

How to communicate your
data story using visuals

For a data story to create impact, tell it to others.

This chapter looks at how to tell data stories visually (as most data stories are told this way). As mentioned in the **Introduction**, this book doesn't cover best-practice data visualisation. Check out page 376 for some great data visualisation resources.

As described in **Chapter 1: Why Visualise Your Data?**, the visuals used to tell data stories are known as **Educate** visuals. These visuals aren't the data story itself but rather its medium of communication (or how it's told).

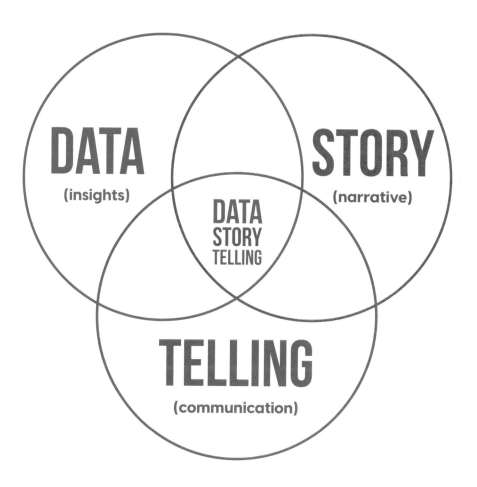

Share your data story in a format that your audience is happy to receive.

A data story is communicated the same way as any other message. Your audience and the amount of detail you're communicating will determine how you tell your data story.

Regardless of the medium through which a data story is shared, it will likely be accompanied by data visuals. Data visuals are often used to help tell a data story.

How Many Data Visuals Does One Data Story Need?

The number of data visuals needed to tell a data story depends on two things:

1. **The data story** (covered in **Chapter 5: The Data Story**)

   The purpose of an **Educate** visual is to help an audience understand the data story. However, if the data visual doesn't aid this understanding, it dilutes (or worse, confuses) the message. Therefore, data visuals should not be shared as part of a data story unless they help to tell it.

2. **The audience** (covered in **Chapter 4: The Audience**)

   Not everyone likes looking at data visualisations.

   I'll just let that sink in.

   Chances are (because you're reading this book) you have an interest in data visualisation as well as data storytelling. But, there are others who will actively avoid using a data visual to understand information. So, don't serve up pages of data visuals to this audience. Tell your data story in the way your audience wants to receive it.

The data visuals you create are guided by your data story's narrative structure.

Using this structure, your story is split into three acts (agreement, contrast, and consequence). Identify the acts of your data story that an audience might need a data visual to help understand. Not every act of a data story needs a data visual—but some acts might need multiple visuals to help explain them.

Data stories can be told using no visuals (see **Chapter 2: Why Tell Stories with Your Data?**), one visual, or multiple visuals. Check out the next page for some examples.

_____
_____
_____
_____

and _____
_____
_____

The **And, But, Therefore (ABT)** data story structure on <u>this page</u> is supported by a data visual in the first act.

The ABT data story structure on the <u>next page</u> is supported by multiple data visuals.

but _____
_____
_____
_____
_____

therefore ___
_____
_____
_____
_____

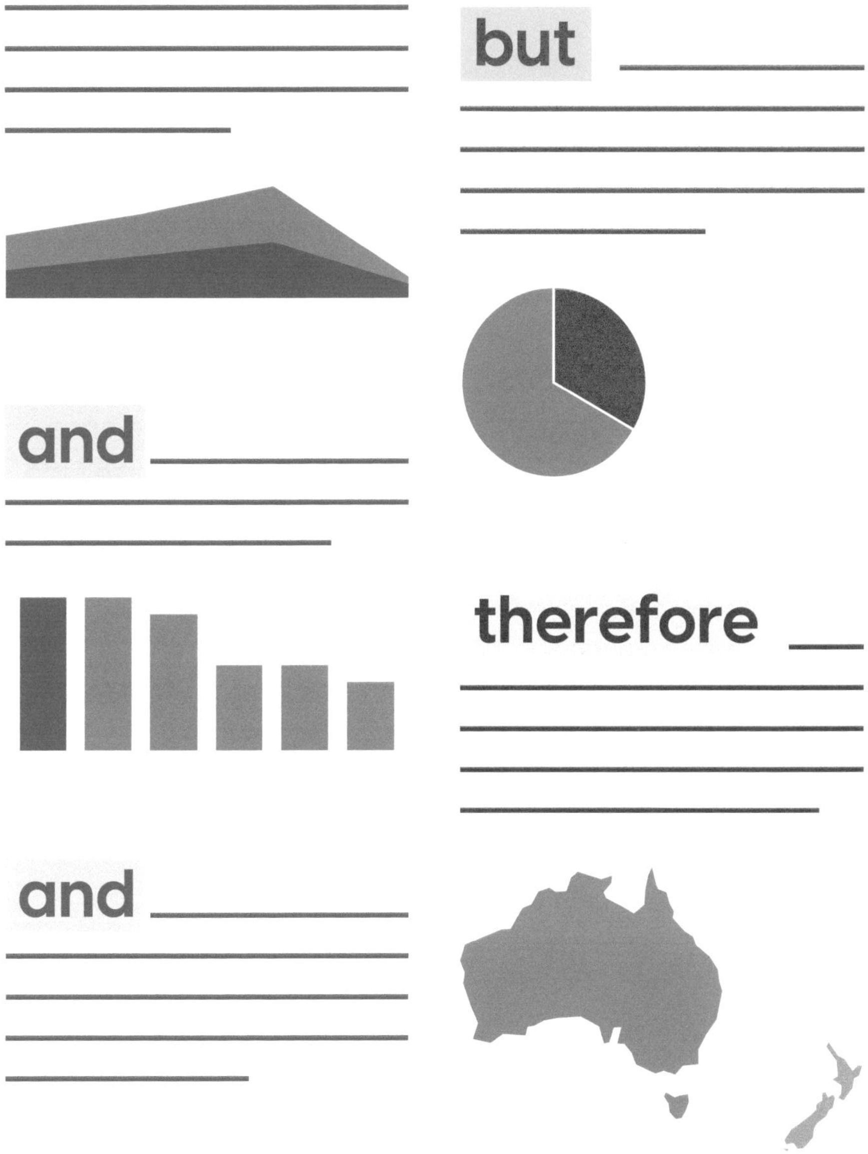

_____
_____
_____
_____

and _____
_____
_____

but _____
_____
_____
_____

therefore __
_____
_____
_____
_____

and _____
_____
_____
_____

Data visuals are often used to help tell a data story.

Data visuals might be shown as part of a presentation, included in a report, or even shared on social media. Despite being commonly mistaken for the data story itself, data visuals are instead a medium of communication. You can't, therefore, create an effective data storytelling visual without first understanding the data story.

Before designing your **Educate** visual, understand what part of your data story it's helping support. To help an audience connect your data visual to your data story, ask yourself the following questions:

1. What's my data visual's takeaway?

2. How can my data visual's design highlight its takeaway?

What's My Data Visual's Takeaway?

Your data visual's takeaway is driven by your data story.

It's hard to create an **Educate** visual if you're not clear on the message you want your audience to take away. This is why it's important to understand your data story before you start designing visuals to communicate it.

Often, your data visual's takeaway has been written as part of your data story. To make it clear to your audience, use the title of your data visual to spell out this takeaway. This is known as a *Takeaway Title*.

A *Takeaway Title* can be a summarised form of your data story or focus on a specific part of it. Either way, it should be kept short and to the point.

How Tania finds her *Takeaway Title*

Tania wrote the following *nested* data story on page 283 and wants to use data visuals to tell it:

Last year, our website sales generated $1 million in revenue. HOWEVER, this year, we increased our social media presence and marketing activity to drive more traffic to the website and boost our website sales. SO, due to these efforts, our website sales revenue doubled. Website sales now generate $2 million a year and account for 25% of total sales revenue.

Before creating her data visual, Tania determines what message she wants her audience to take away from her data visual (also known as her *Takeaway Title*):

In the last year, our website sales revenue doubled.

After identifying her takeaway, Tania can design a data visual to best communicate it. The data visual she uses to communicate her data story might be different from the data visual she used to analyse the data.

DATA VISUALS SHOULD **NOT** BE SHARED AS PART OF A **DATA STORY** UNLESS THEY HELP TO TELL IT.

How Can My Design Highlight My Takeaway?

Data storytelling involves contrast.

In general, contrast means noticing the differences between things. In data storytelling, like in other forms of storytelling, contrast is really important.

Data storytelling contrast can be introduced in various ways, from data metrics and narrative structure (both covered in **Chapter 5: The Data Story**) to the visuals used to help tell the data story.

Visual contrast helps highlight the takeaway of your data visual. It focuses an audience on the part of the data visual referred to in the takeaway title. If applied correctly, your audience notices what you want them to see before they realise they're looking for it. This lessens their mental load as they don't need to search for this meaning themselves.

The next few pages detail different ways to add visual contrast. Varying the hue, weight, value, and size of specific elements in your data visual creates not only a clear focus for the audience, but also a clear pathway.

DATA STORYTELLING CONTRAST

Data contrast

Data contrast (comparing data measurements) helps convey the data's significance.

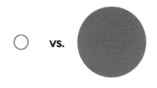

Story (narrative) contrast

Narrative tension drives the progression of a story and helps engage an audience.

Visual contrast

Visual contrast directs an audience's attention. It helps draw focus to the most important parts of your visual.

VISUAL CONTRAST

Hue

Hue is the property of a colour that allows it to be distinguished from others. It's what makes it red, blue, etc.

Colours are organised on a colour wheel with primary colours (red, blue, yellow) as the foundation for creating all other colours. A colour's hue is determined by its position on the colour wheel.

Colours with more distance from each other on the wheel will show higher contrast when compared. For example, blue and orange have more visual contrast than yellow and orange. Colours with the highest contrast are known as complementary colours and are located opposite each other on the colour wheel.

Black and white are known as achromatic colours, meaning they are without hue. Visual contrast can be seen between colours on the wheel or when one colour is used with achromatic colours.

COLOUR WHEEL

● Primary colour

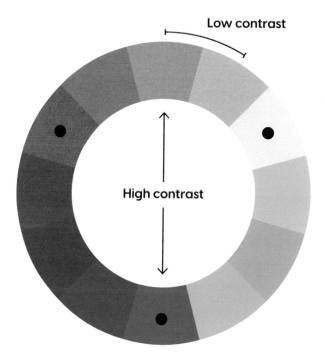

It's important to recognise that people see colour differently.

There are many books that focus on design accessibility, so I won't be going in-depth here. It is important to keep in mind that red-green colour blindness is the most common variety of colour deficiency in humans. This means that while red-green colour combinations are often used to create data visuals, audience members with red-green colour blindness will struggle to differentiate between these two colours. So, if you create a data visual using a traffic-light colour palette, your audience might not be able to separate the extremes.

This colour accessibility problem is commonly seen when designing **Inform** (or dashboard) visuals, rather than **Educate** (data storytelling) visuals—see **Chapter 1: Why Visualise Your Data?** for more about these two types of data visuals. Many dashboards are inaccessible to some people because they use red (to highlight negative data values) and green (to highlight positive data values) in the same data visual.

The nature of an **Educate** visual makes it easier to avoid combining these two colours. The choice and placement of colour are determined by the data story. You pick the colour that communicates your message—red to highlight a negative takeaway or green for a positive takeaway.

VISUAL CONTRAST

Weight

The weight of a font or line refers to how heavy it is.

The larger the weight difference between fonts or lines, the more contrast they show when compared to each other.

Bold fonts have a heavier weight than light fonts.

Bold Font   Light Font

Thick lines have a heavier weight than thin lines.

A heavyweight font or line will stand out from a lighter one. Heavier weights can help highlight important elements in a data visual.

VISUAL CONTRAST

Value

The value of a colour refers to how light or dark it is.

Light colours have a high value; dark colours have a low value. For example, yellow has a higher value than brown, so these colours show a noticeable amount of visual contrast when compared to each other.

Lower value   Higher value

The value of a colour decreases by adding black (changing its shade) or increases by adding white (changing its tint). The larger the value difference between colours, the more contrast they show compared to each other.

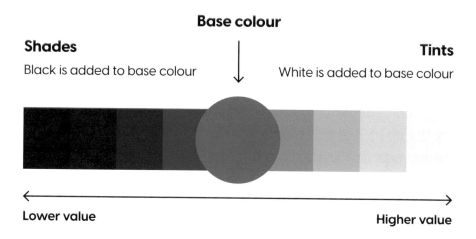

Base colour

Shades
Black is added to base colour

Tints
White is added to base colour

Lower value

Higher value

The further a shade or tint is from its base colour, the more contrast can be seen between them. Colour shades and tints can help you add visual contrast without needing to stray too far from brand colour palettes.

Lower value

Higher value

VISUAL CONTRAST

Size

The main elements of a data visual are usually determined by the data, but there are visual elements (mainly text) whose size isn't linked to a data measurement.

The size of the following text elements is subject to a Data Storyteller's discretion:

- Title
- Subtitle
- Legend
- Axis label and value
- Data label and value
- Annotations

Contrasting larger text against smaller text helps create a visual hierarchy within your data visual. By understanding that larger text will be read before the smaller text, you can use text size to create a pathway for people to understand your data visual.

You'll read this last (if at all).

YOU WILL READ THIS FIRST.

And then you'll probably read this next.

You might then skim-read this paragraph without paying too much attention to its content. Did you notice the sentence above the word "YOU"?

Visual contrast (combined with a data story) simplifies the process of understanding information.

It's important to note that visual contrast doesn't necessarily simplify the information, but rather how an audience processes it. Your design helps them navigate the best way to understand the information.

But for any visual contrast to be effective, you need to be clear on the takeaway you're communicating. This will help you decide what to visually contrast to tell your data story.

THE **MORE** DESIGN CONTRAST **YOU TRY** TO **ADD**, THE **LESS** YOU **END UP HAVING**.

BE CLEAR ON THE MESSAGE YOU'RE HIGHLIGHTING.

Unless your audience is invested in understanding your data visual, you'll need to make it as easy as possible for them.

Here are five steps to creating an effective **Educate** data visual to support your takeaway:

1. **Identify the data metric(s) that supports your takeaway.**
    Your takeaway will likely focus on a specific data metric (or metrics), and this is what you need to visualise. Think of this data metric as the evidence for your takeaway.

2. **Determine what data measurements you need to visualise.** If you show too much data, you create noise (a distraction from your takeaway). However, if you show too little data, your audience questions the significance of it. The amount of data you need to show depends on what it takes for your audience to trust your takeaway.

3. **Choose a chart type that visualises the data metric in a way that supports your takeaway.**

   How your data metric supports your takeaway will determine the best chart type. For example, is it better to show the data metric over time or between categories? These two ways to represent the data will likely require different chart types.

4. **Add visual contrast to focus a reader on your takeaway.**

   Although your data metric and chart type work together to support your takeaway, not all parts of your data visual are equally important when communicating this. There will likely be specific parts (usually data measurements) that provide the key supporting evidence for your takeaway. Using visual contrast to highlight these helps an audience navigate your data visual.

5. Add annotations to explain further details.

There might be times when there are multiple takeaways you'd like to add to the title of your data visual, but try to refrain from doing this. In these situations, use annotations to provide the details that don't fit into a title. Let your title communicate one key takeaway and annotate any other supporting details. This creates a hierarchy of your information and simplifies an audience's experience. An annotated data visual encourages further engagement to learn more.

How Tania designs her data visual

After clarifying her takeaway (page 305), Tania works through the steps from the previous pages.

1. **Identify the data metric(s) that supports your takeaway.** Tania's takeaway focuses on website sales revenue so she visualises this metric.

2. **Determine what data measurements you need to visualise.** Tania's takeaway compares data measurements for the last two years. However, she knows that only showing this data might cause her audience to question if the increase is just following historical trends. So, Tania includes data from previous years for context.

3. **Choose a chart type that visualises the data measurements in a way that supports your takeaway.** Tania is visualising data for one metric across multiple years. To keep it simple, she could use either a line or a bar chart. Because her takeaway focuses on the relative difference between years, Tania feels a bar chart would allow her to add stronger visual contrast, despite using a line graph to initially analyse the data.

4. **Add visual contrast to focus a reader on your takeaway.** With a less-is-more approach, Tania uses colour value to highlight the bar representing the most recent year's data measurement.

5. **Add annotations to explain further details.** Tania's takeaway highlights the increase in website sales revenue, but she uses annotations to help explain this increase and tell more of her data story.

On the next page is Tania's written data story and the data visual she created to communicate it. Her annotations don't follow the data story word for word, as the data visual communicates some of this information.

Her data visual also doesn't tell all of the data story—just her takeaway. Tania reads the data story when she presents and shares the data visual to support her key takeaway.

Last year, our website sales generated $1 million in revenue. HOWEVER, this year, we increased our social media presence and marketing activity to drive more traffic to the website and boost our website sales. SO, due to these efforts, our website sales revenue doubled. Website sales now generate $2 million a year and account for 25% of total sales revenue.

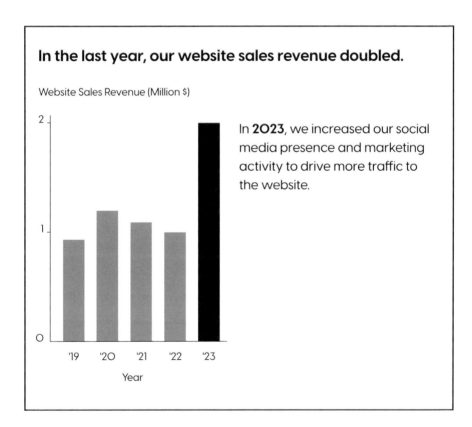

In the last year, our website sales revenue doubled.

Website Sales Revenue (Million $)

In **2023**, we increased our social media presence and marketing activity to drive more traffic to the website.

Year

Using data visuals to tell a data story has its advantages.

- **Data visuals make data measurements easier to compare.** Visualising data allows someone to leverage their pattern recognition skills, leading to a quicker understanding of the data and insights.

- **Data visuals cut through data complexity.** Visualisations help to summarise complex data, providing the audience with an overall understanding as opposed to getting lost in the data details.

- **Data visuals highlight what's important.** Through the addition of visual contrast, data visuals help guide an audience to focus on what matters most in the data.

- **Data visuals help make a data story memorable.** Visuals are known for improving memory because we're better at processing and remembering visual information (compared to text).

- **Data visuals provide visual evidence to support the data story.** An audience can see the data, making the communication more convincing than relying solely on the written data story.

Emotive Elements

Emotive elements help enrich an audience's understanding and connection with the data.

You might not immediately associate data communication with evoking emotion, but sometimes, these emotions make a data story more engaging and relatable.

Emotive elements help to humanise data, creating a strong emotional connection between the audience and the real world that data represents. These elements range from the use of <u>powerful</u> images and the <u>strategic</u> selection of colours to the <u>careful</u> choice of words and personal stories.

The type of emotion an element evokes can differ depending on the culture or society of the audience. For example, in many cultures, the colour red is associated with emotions like passion, danger, or anger. In other cultures, red is associated with happiness and good luck.

HOW I'VE USED EMOTIVE ELEMENTS IN THIS BOOK

Images

My vision for this book was a "kids' book for adults". Children's books feel friendly and are designed to evoke joy in their readers—which is what I wanted you to feel when reading this book. For a different way to use images to tell a data story, check out **Chapter 7: The Practice**.

Colours

I've used four main chromatic colours (**red**, **blue**, **yellow**, and **green**). These are designed to evoke a sense of simplicity and ease of understanding, complementing the book's images.

Words

The words underlined on the previous page are examples of emotive words. You might have noticed that the book's character stories contain more emotive words than its more technical sections.

Personal stories

The character stories aim to evoke empathy for what the character is experiencing. Maybe you've been in a similar situation and can relate?

Despite its potential to engage the audience, using excessive emotion in data storytelling can introduce bias.

While emotive elements in data storytelling can create a powerful connection with an audience, approach their use with caution. The emotive elements you use will depend on your data story and audience.

Being overly emotional in the way you communicate data can suggest a bias and lead others to question your objectivity. It's important to strike a balance between conveying the human element and maintaining credibility.

Keep It Honest

Ask yourself these questions to help your data storytelling remain as unbiased as possible.

- **Have I selected a good range of data measurements?**
  As mentioned on page 320, there's a fine line between including too many data measurements (creating data noise) and too few data measurements (causing suspicions of cherry-picking). Try to anticipate any points of friction from your audience (or reasons preventing them from accepting your data story). Don't leave your audience guessing the context of your data measurements.

- **Is my data accurately represented by my data visual?**
  Following best-practice data visualisation guidelines when designing Educate visuals is a great start. These are seen by many as guidelines (rather than hard rules), as there will always be exceptions. However, before diverting from best practice, understand why it's encouraged. For example, be careful visualising data on a dual axis or truncating your y-axis, as these can mislead an audience (even if that wasn't your intention). Check out some great data visualisation resources on page 376.

- **Does my data visual reflect the accuracy of my data?**
  For example, don't use multiple decimal places to display data measurements if your analysis hasn't generated this

level of accuracy. Or, at the other end of the scale, don't round up to unreasonable larger values.

- **Can my audience understand my data visual?** Some chart types are widely understood. The majority of audiences know how to read a bar, line, or pie chart. These make them good chart types to use when communicating to more general audiences. The data literacy of your audience (their ability to read and interpret a data visual) should determine many of your design decisions.

- **Is my *Takeaway Title* overly sensational?** While it's important to convey the seriousness of certain issues or evoke an emotional response from certain audiences, try to avoid creating visuals that overly sensationalise. For example, data visuals used for political promotion often exaggerate the importance of the data insight. Sensationalised data visuals designed to induce fear have been shown to lead to panic and/or misinformation.

- **Does my takeaway and data visual support my data story?** Your data visual has one job—to help communicate all or part of your data story. If your takeaway or the data you're visualising has nothing to do with your data story, it's not helping you.

A data storytelling visual always supports something bigger: its data story.

You can't create an effective data storytelling visual without first understanding the data story.

When designing these data visuals, your aim should extend beyond simply creating something beautiful. While a visually appealing data visual is undoubtedly valuable, this beauty should not come at the expense of effective communication. The goal of a data storytelling visual is to guide an audience through their understanding of the data story.

A data story is often told using a mix of verbal, written, and visual ways of communication.

DATA STORYTELLING DESIGN DECISIONS SHOULD BE FIRST FILTERED THROUGH A LENS OF EFFECTIVE COMMUNICATION.

CHAPTER 7

The Practice

Bringing it all together

"But, how does it all work in practice?"

Let's take a look.

This book is your guide to the end-to-end data storytelling process. However, if you want to start in the middle, that's okay. Your data storytelling practice might not require all of the steps covered in the book. Maybe you have a good understanding of your business goal and audience; if so, then go straight to creating your data story.

Regardless of how you dip in and out of the process, the next section shows how all the frameworks in this book have been used to create and tell a specific data story.

Humanity Is Ageing

How I created a detailed data story

Completing the **PGAI Framework** helped me clarify my need to communicate—or better understand the world the data story will exist in.

Problem What is the world struggling with?

There are negative consequences to the global human population growing older.

Goal What outcome would minimise the problem?

more people understand the consequences of an ageing population and why it's important to address them.

Action What did I do to achieve the goal?

Research into global ageing populations (with a focus on New Zealand).

What are you using data storytelling for?

☐ To influence the action   ☺ To share the action

Impact What value could the action create?

People are engaged in national planning discussions around retirement age, migration, education, and healthcare.

This **Stakeholder Matrix** prioritises my potential audience groups to help me achieve the previous goal.

High Influence

Satisfy media Elected officials	**Engage** Government agencies and policymakers National healthcare and education planners

Low Interest ← → **High Interest**

Update Employers Temporary residents Younger generations	**Inform** Rest homes People nearing retirement age Entrepreneurs

Low Influence

The below **User Stories** help to understand an audience group's potential motivation to learn more about ageing populations.

As <u>someone new to working in a government agency</u>, **I want** to learn about the consequences of an ageing population **so that** I can take a more holistic approach to my work.

As an <u>elected official</u>, **I want** to know how New Zealand's population compares to other countries **so that** I can better understand the urgency of any solutions.

As a <u>policymaker</u>, **I want** to understand the challenges and opportunities associated with ageing populations **so that** I can develop effective policies and programs that address the needs of elderly citizens and ensure their quality of life.

As an <u>entrepreneur</u>, **I want** to learn about ageing populations **so that** I can identify potential market opportunities to meet the needs and preferences of older consumers.

As <u>someone approaching retirement age</u>, **I want** to educate myself about ageing populations **so that** I can plan for my own future and make informed decisions about healthcare, finances, and lifestyle choices.

The below **Empathy Spectrums** help me (the Data Storyteller) understand the communication preferences of an audience new to working in a government agency (the first *User Story*).

How well do they/I understand this topic?

Novice Them   Me   Expert

How do they/I prefer to be communicated with about this?

Summary   Them   Me   Detail

How are they/I likely to react to my message?

Spontaneous   Them   Me   Thoughtful

How interested are they/I to receive this information?

Low interest   Them   Me   High interest

The *Time Data Story Canvas* helps arrange my data story building blocks.

1. Data Metric What **Data Metric** is changing?	2. Character Whom (or what) does the **Data Metric** describe?
Life expectancy (global)	Global human population

3. Times	Time 1	Time 2
Select two time points when the **Data Metric** will be measured (to highlight its change).	1960	2021

4. Data Change	Data (Time 1)	Data (Time 2)
Record the **Data Metric's** measurements at **Times** 1 and 2.	47.7 years	71.0 years
Calculate the difference between data measurements (or the **Data Metric's** change).	**Change** +23.3 years	

5. Character Change (an expression)

Times + Character + Data Metric + Data Change

In the 61 years between 1960 and 2021, the life expectancy of the global human population rose by 23.3 years.

6. Impact How was the **Character** impacted by the **Data Change**?

☑ Positively   ☐ No change   ☑ Negatively

7. Reason Why did the **Character Change** happen?

People are living longer (improved healthcare) and having fewer children (education and employment opportunities).

8. Unknowns What don't you know about the **Character Change**?

What did COVID-19 teach us about vulnerable populations? Can governments support more people with fewer tax payers?

9. Reaction How do you respond to the **Character Change**?

What was learned from **Reason**?	What can be done to remove **Unknowns**?	What can be done to improve **Impact**?
multiple factors contribute to life expectancy	understand how COVID-19 impacted different groups	migration settings New technology Global cooperation

10. Context What else does your audience need to know to understand the **Character Change**?

Fewer people born may be good for the climate.
It's important for governments and communities to find ways to support and care for older people.

The below data story was written for an audience new to working in a government agency. It combines information from my previous *PGAI Framework* and *Time Data Story Canvas*. It's a *summary* data story written in a three-act structure, using the **ABT Framework**.

Summary Data Story

Summary Act 1   The global population is growing older, AND around the world, people are living longer and having fewer children.

Summary Act 2   HOWEVER, while fewer people born may be good for the climate, there are consequences of an ageing population that governments need to consider.

Summary Act 3   THEREFORE, as the population ages, it's important for governments and communities to find ways to support and care for older people.

My next step is to expand the *summary* data story because it doesn't give my audience the detail they need.

My *summary* data story sets the scope of what I'll communicate. I choose the below topics from my *Data Story Canvas* to help add further detail. Each of these topics will become a *nested* data story. Although the *summary* data story is global, my *nested* data stories focus on New Zealand's ageing population.

Act 1 Nested Data Story

 New Zealand's ageing population

Act 2 Nested Data Stories

 Healthcare   Financial support

Act 3 Nested Data Stories

 Migration   Technology

 Learning from other countries

Each *nested* data story goes through the same creation process using the *Data Story Canvas* and three-act narrative structure. As the *nested* data stories are designed for the same purpose and audience as the *summary* data story, these aspects remain the same.

Given the varying levels of data literacy within this broad audience, the data stories aren't data-complex or data-heavy. For example, where possible, proportions are shown in terms of people (one in three people) rather than percentages (33%).

The next few pages show the narrative structure of the *nested* data stories, along with their data sources (something to track when using multiple sources). The migration *nested* data story (page 352) has *nested* data stories of its own.

Act 1 Nested ABT

> New Zealand's ageing population

New Zealand's population is also ageing. A person born in New Zealand today is expected to live for more than 80 years. That's over a decade longer than people born in 1960.

AND while the average New Zealand woman had four children in 1960... today, she has two.

BUT, these changes in demographics reflect positive things. Improved healthcare and living conditions help people live longer. Empowerment of women allows them to pursue careers. Education and employment opportunities mean women delay having children.

THEREFORE, an ageing population is often seen as a sign of a healthy society.

Data
ourworldindata.org/life-expectancy
ourworldindata.org/fertility-rate

Act 2 Nested Data Story

Healthcare

As people age, they are more likely to have ongoing health issues that require medical care. One in three deaths in New Zealand are caused by heart disease. One in four people in New Zealand will die with dementia.

BUT, ageing populations can put a strain on healthcare systems, as seen during the COVID-19 pandemic. In New Zealand, 95% of deaths related to COVID-19 occurred among people over the age of 60.

THEREFORE, to meet the growing demand for care, there will be a need for more healthcare workers, including doctors, nurses, and caregivers.

Data
heartfoundation.org.nz/statistics
alzheimers.org.nz
health.govt.nz

Act 2 Nested Data Story

Financial support

In 1960, there were six working-age people for every retired person in New Zealand. Today, that ratio is four-to-one. In 2060, that ratio is projected to be two-to-one. Over time, there will be fewer people paying taxes and more people receiving a pension. In 2060, 27% of New Zealanders will be eligible for the pension (up from 16% in 2023).

The New Zealand pension helps people maintain a basic standard of living in retirement, BUT many people still need additional income in order to maintain their desired lifestyle. For every five older renters, two will pay more than 80 cents of every pension dollar to their landlords.

AS A RESULT, many New Zealanders feel they won't have enough money to retire unless they continue working past the age of 65.

Data

ourworldindata.org/age-structure

retirement.govt.nz (Retirement Income Policy Review 2022)

Act 3 Nested Data Story

Migration

Migration is the permanent movement of people from one place to another. It's used by countries to help compensate for falling birth rates.

NESTED

Younger people move to cities for job opportunities and access to higher education.

BUT, older people approaching retirement can also influence migration by moving to smaller towns that fit their preferred lifestyle.

AS A RESULT, cities usually have younger people living in them, while smaller towns and rural areas have more older people.

BUT, in recent years, the COVID-19 pandemic has altered this balance.

NESTED

> In 2022, the number of people living in Auckland decreased for the second year in a row. More people moved out of the city to live in other parts of New Zealand. Auckland's population decline is usually offset by people arriving from other countries.
>
> HOWEVER, the COVID-19 pandemic had a major impact on the way people move around the world. Between 2021 and 2022, there were nearly 9,000 fewer people living and working in Auckland.
>
> Auckland businesses struggled to find enough workers to meet demand, driving the New Zealand government to modify its immigration policies in response to the new realities of the pandemic.

Migration can, THEREFORE, significantly impact the demographics of a region.

Data
stuff.co.nz (Welcome to the hyperageing nation that is New Zealand)
stats.govt.nz (Regional population growth slows)

Act 3 Nested Data Story

Technology

Communication technologies help older people stay connected with loved ones, reducing loneliness and social isolation. In New Zealand, one in three people over 65 years reported feeling lonely in 2021. Wearable devices track health indicators and help with the early detection of diseases. Smart home technologies allow older people to live independently in their own homes.

YET, there are risks to consider when using technology. If healthcare technology malfunctions, this can be dangerous. If personal information is misused online, this can be harmful. Technology can be expensive, making it difficult for some to access. It's estimated one in three older people in New Zealand do not use the internet.

It's THEREFORE important to consider both the benefits and risks of using technology to support older people in maintaining their health and well-being.

Data

stats.govt.nz (New Zealanders' mental wellbeing declines)

news.anz.com (Digital learning age concern)

Act 3 Nested Data Story

Learning from other countries

A large proportion of Japan's population is elderly. It's estimated that 30% of people living in Japan are 65 years or older. Japan's proportion of elderly is significantly higher than other countries (such as New Zealand, where in 2021 only 16% of the population was 65 or older).

HOWEVER, this hyper-aged society has its challenges, which the government of Japan is addressing with various initiatives. Japan aims to increase workforce participation of women and the elderly, improve welfare services, and encourage immigration. Japan also recognised that digital transformation is crucial for preparing its healthcare system to serve an ageing population.

CONSEQUENTLY, Japan now has the experience to provide guidance to other countries facing similar demographic shifts.

Data

ourworldindata.org/age-structure

japantimes.co.jp (Japan's graying population)

With my *nested* data stories written and I'm now clear on <u>what</u> I want to communicate, my next step is to consider <u>how</u> to best **tell** the full data story.

It's the job of my public servant audience to support the people represented in my data story, so I'm using visuals to help evoke an emotive response. I want my audience to see their communities in the data. An illustrated style helps portray the reality behind some of the numbers. A comic book format helps make the data story more engaging to read. Combined, these design styles reflect how easy the data story is to understand, making it approachable for my audience. It will also be something different from the many default charts they will undoubtedly see every day.

The full data story is visualised over the next few pages. The visual was created using a combination of the following tools: Midjourney, Procreate, Adobe Photoshop, and Adobe Illustrator. Bar a few headings and closing statements, nothing about the visualised data story differs from what is written on the previous pages. The <u>visual hierarchy</u> helps reflect the <u>data story hierarchy</u>.

Humanity is ageing.

The global population is growing older. Around the world, people are living longer and having fewer children.

New Zealand's population is also ageing.

But these changes in demographics reflect positive things.

Therefore, an ageing population is often seen as a sign of a healthy society.

However, while fewer people born may be good for the climate, there are consequences of an ageing population that governments need to consider.

HEALTHCARE

Governments need to provide healthcare to a larger proportion of the population.

But ageing populations can put a strain on healthcare systems, as seen during the COVID-19 pandemic.

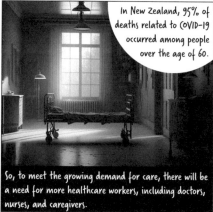

In New Zealand, 95% of deaths related to COVID-19 occurred among people over the age of 60.

So, to meet the growing demand for care, there will be a need for more healthcare workers, including doctors, nurses, and caregivers.

FINANCIAL SUPPORT

As populations age, governments need to support more retirement-aged people.

In 1960, there were six working-age people for every retired person in New Zealand.

1960

Today, that ratio is around four-to-one.

2023

In 2060, that ratio is projected to be two-to-one.

2060

over time, there will be fewer people paying taxes and more people receiving a pension.

In 2060, 27% of New Zealanders will be eligible for the pension (up from 16% in 2021).

The New Zealand pension helps people to maintain a basic standard of living in retirement…

For every five older renters, two will pay 80 cents of every pension dollar to their landlords.

…but many people still need additional income in order to maintain their desired lifestyle.

As a result, many New Zealanders feel they won't have enough money for retirement unless they continue working past the age of 65.

Therefore, as the population ages, it's important for governments and communities to find ways to support and care for older people.

MIGRATION CAN BOOST THE WORKING POPULATION

Migration is the permanent movement of people from one place to another. It's used by countries to help compensate for falling birth rates.

Younger people move to cities for job opportunities and access to higher education.

Older people approaching retirement can also influence migration by moving to smaller towns that fit their preferred lifestyle.

As a result, cities usually have younger people living in them, while smaller towns and rural areas have more older people.

But, in recent years, the COVID-19 pandemic altered this balance.

In 2022, the number of people living in Auckland city decreased for the second year in a row.

More people moved out of Auckland to live in other parts of New Zealand.

Auckland's population decline is usually offset by people arriving from other countries.

However, the COVID-19 pandemic had a major impact on how people move around the world.

Between 2021 and 2022, there were nearly 9,000 fewer people living and working in Auckland.

NATURAL	MIGRATION	POPULATION
Births - Deaths	Arrivals - Departures	Natural & Migration
+12,000		
	−20,900	−8,900

Auckland businesses struggled to find enough workers to meet demand...

... driving the New Zealand government to modify its immigration policies in response to the new realities of the pandemic.

Migration can therefore significantly impact the demographics of a region.

TECHNOLOGY CAN HELP SUPPORT OLDER PEOPLE

Digital tools and services enable people to maintain their health and well-being.

Communication technologies help older people stay connected with loved ones, reducing loneliness and social isolation.

In New Zealand, one in three people over 65 years reported feeling lonely in 2021.

Wearable devices track health indicators and help with the early detection of diseases.

Smart home technologies allow older people to live independently in their own homes.

Yet, there are risks to consider when using technology.

If healthcare technology malfunctions, this can be dangerous.

If personal information is misused online, this can be harmful.

Technology can be expensive, making it difficult for some to access.

It's estimated, one in three older people in New Zealand do not use the Internet.

It's therefore important to consider both the benefits and risks of using technology to support older people in maintaining their health and well-being.

COUNTRIES CAN LEARN FROM EACH OTHER

A large proportion of Japan's population is elderly.

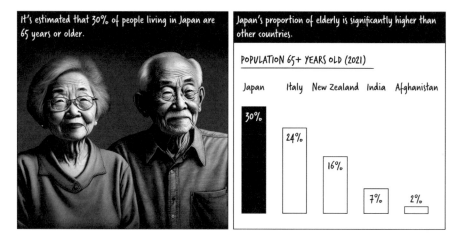

It's estimated that 30% of people living in Japan are 65 years or older.

Japan's proportion of elderly is significantly higher than other countries.

POPULATION 65+ YEARS OLD (2021)

Japan — 30%
Italy — 24%
New Zealand — 16%
India — 7%
Afghanistan — 2%

This hyper-aged society has its challenges which the government of Japan is addressing with various initiatives.

Japan aims to increase workforce participation of women and the elderly, improve welfare services, and encourage immigration.

Japan also recognised that digital transformation is crucial for preparing its healthcare system to serve an ageing population.

Consequently, Japan has the experience to provide guidance to other countries facing similar demographic shifts.

As we age, we have the opportunity not only to look back on the past, but to actively shape our future.

Governments play a vital role in how this future looks.

Practice

There is only so much you can learn from reading this book.

The first two chapters (**Chapter 1: Why Visualise Your Data?** and **Chapter 2: Why Tell Stories with Your Data?**) are the context (or Know) chapters. They help you understand where data storytelling fits into the world of data visualisation and the world of business.

Chapters 3 to 6 are the practical (or How) chapters. They detail my data storytelling process. I've left nothing out. You will learn how to find, write, and tell data stories that resonate with your chosen audience to create business impact. However, you won't develop your data storytelling skills unless you apply these learnings. In other words, you need to practice.

The following pages suggest easy ways to practice (or Do) the process covered in the previous practical chapters. You can download templates for all data storytelling frameworks at roguepenguin.co.nz/book/downloads

How to practice Chapter 3: The Business

Ask yourself the following questions to determine the business goal hierarchy you're working within:

- What is something you're either working on or want to work on? This is your **action**.
- What is your action trying to achieve? This is your **goal**.
- What other actions would also help to achieve your goal?
- What are wider goals and actions your goal will help drive?

Using your above action and goal, complete your **Problem-Goal-Action-Impact (PGAI) Framework** (page 141).

- Use your goal to help identify your business **problem**.
- The **impact** of your action is closely linked to the next goal(s) in your business goal hierarchy.

How to practice Chapter 4: The Audience

Consider your *PGAI Framework* on the previous page. Ask yourself the following questions to determine whom you would want or need to communicate with:

- Who is also trying to achieve your goal?

- Who is responsible for (or impacted by) the actions/goals at levels above yours?

- Are some of these audience groups outside your organisation?

Complete a **Stakeholder Matrix** (page 156) to help prioritise your audience groups.

Choose an audience group from your *Stakeholder Matrix* and write as many **User Stories** (page 164) for them as you can.

Plot your chosen audience group on each of the four **Empathy Spectrums** (page 171). How do they differ from where you fall on these spectrums?

How to practice Chapter 5: The Data Story

Find and write a data story

1. Select a <u>data metric</u> you're interested in.

2. Whose information is it measuring? This is your <u>character</u>.

3. Are the data metric's measurements changing over time for your character? If so, this creates a *Time* data story (page 206).

    Are your character's data measurements different from another character's? This creates a *Character* data story (page 207).

4. Complete the appropriate **Data Story Canvas** for the data story you want to create.

5. Arrange your canvas building blocks into a three-act structure using the **And-But-Therefore (ABT) Framework** (page 256). This is your <u>data story</u>.

6. Could you present this data story visually?

Write <u>your</u> story

Arrange the information in your *PGAI Framework* (page 369) into a three-act structure using the *ABT Framework*.

This will help you create your elevator pitch (the story of why you do the work you do). It will make it easier to talk to others about the work you're doing and the impact you hope to create. You can read mine on page 257.

How to practice Chapter 6: The Telling

An **Educate** visual's title is driven by the data story it helps tell. If you're unfamiliar with creating this type of visual, here's an easy way to practice (without having to write a data story):

1. Choose a graph. It can be any graph you like.

2. Write down all the takeaway messages you can see in it.

3. Can you group any of these takeaways? If so, summarise them into one key message.

4. Choose a takeaway you want to focus on. This will become your new visual's *Takeaway Title* (page 304).

5. Using your starting graph's data, design a new data visual that best communicates your *Takeaway Title*. It doesn't have to be the same chart type as your original graph.

6. Use **design contrast** (page 308) to highlight the most important part of your new data visual (the part that best supports your *Takeaway Title*).

7. Are there any other parts of your data visual you can explain further using annotations? Only do this if they are relevant to your *Takeaway Title*.

"WRITERS WRITE. RUNNERS RUN. ESTABLISH YOUR IDENTITY BY DOING YOUR WORK."

SETH GODIN, THE PRACTICE

THIS IS YOUR HANDBOOK.

Other Data Visualisation and Data Storytelling Books

This list is by no means exhaustive, but it offers a potential next step for some reading direction.

Avoiding Data Pitfalls Ben Jones

Better Data Visualizations Jonathan Schwabish

Building Science Graphics Jen Christiansen

Chart Spark Alli Torban

ColorWise Kate Strachnyi

Data Sketches Nadieh Bremer, Shirley Wu

Data Visualisation Andy Kirk

Data Visualization: A Practical Introduction Kieran Healy

Data Visualization Made Simple Kristen Sosulski

Dear Data Giorgia Lupi, Stefanie Posavec

Effective Data Storytelling Brent Dykes

Effective Data Visualization Stephanie Evergreen

Everyday Business Storytelling Janine Kurnoff, Lee Lazarus

Good Charts Scott Berinato

Houston, We Have a Narrative Randy Olson

I'm Not a Numbers Person Dr. Selena Fisk

Information Is Beautiful David McCandless

Info We Trust RJ Andrews

Joyful Infographics Nigel Holmes

#MakeoverMonday Andy Kriebel, Eva Murray

Making Numbers Count Chip Heath, Karla Starr

Practical Charts Nicholas P. Desbarats

Present Beyond Measure Lea Pica

Questions in Dataviz Neil Richards

Resonate Nancy Duarte

Storytelling With Charts Sam Schreim

Storytelling With Data Cole Nussbaumer Knaflic

The Art of Insight Alberto Cairo

The Big Picture Steve Wexler

The Story of Colour Gavin Evans

The Visual Display of Quantitative Information Edward R. Tufte

Visualization Analysis and Design Tamara Munzner

We Are Here Chris McDowall, Tim Denee

How to Support This Book

Thank you for purchasing this book! I hope it was fun to read and it's proven so useful that you keep coming back to it.

The marketing strategy for this book has been grassroots. There is no budget from a big publisher. If you'd like to join my marketing team (and I'd be thrilled to have you on board), here are a few ways you can help to share this book's story:

Leave a review

Your opinion matters! Your review could be the deciding factor for someone considering if the book is right for them. Popular book review sites include <u>Amazon</u> and <u>Goodreads</u>.

Share how you're using it

Have you had any "a-ha" moments while reading? Share your experiences! This is a great way to inspire others and get them excited about data storytelling. The book's design also makes it easy to share your highlights on social media.

I'd love to hear how you've used this book and what you think of it. You can contact me at <u>kat@roguepenguin.co.nz</u>

Give the book as a gift

Do you know someone who would appreciate some data storytelling wisdom? Gifting the book to a friend or family member is a thoughtful gesture that can lead to some great discussions and personal growth.

Bulk buy for your team

If you're excited about what you've found in the book, why not take your whole team on a learning adventure? Grabbing a bunch of copies can be a game-changer for everyone, encouraging fresh ideas and collaboration.

Attend a workshop

Looking for a more immersive and hands-on learning experience? Book the team on the workshop that served as the foundation for this book. Rogue Penguin workshops are an excellent way to dive deeper into the concepts and techniques discussed in these pages and receive personalised guidance. You can find out more at roguepenguin.co.nz

Together, we can help others discover the power of effective data storytelling and create a positive impact in their field. Thank you again for being a part of this journey with me!

About the Author

Kat Greenbrook is a Data Storyteller from Aotearoa, New Zealand. She is a consultant, workshop facilitator, industry speaker, and founder of the data storytelling company, Rogue Penguin.

In 2002, Kat graduated from Massey University with a science degree. Unsatisfied with pursuing a career as a scientist, she opted for a more business-focused path. This led her to the field of data analytics. Over the next ten years, Kat held technical data roles spanning a wide array of sectors, including banking, energy, education, e-commerce, FMCG, telecommunications, tourism, and government. As an analyst, she gained invaluable insights into the communication challenges faced by people in these roles.

In 2015, Kat completed a digital design degree, blending her design and data analytics expertise. This put her at the forefront of the burgeoning field of data visualisation, which would later evolve to encompass data storytelling. This pivotal moment paved the way for her to establish Rogue Penguin in 2016, a company dedicated to bridging the gap between analytics and business operations.

Today, Kat's engaging data storytelling workshops attract professionals from various fields, including data science, communications, accounting, marketing, and graphic design. She holds several government training contracts and a position on the training roster for the United Nations System Staff College (UNSSC). In addition to her consulting work, Kat is highly regarded as an industry speaker and frequently shares her expertise by guest lecturing at universities.

Kat has pushed data communication boundaries throughout her career. With a unique blend of science, business, and design, she empowers data professionals to communicate data effectively, illustrating the transformative potential of combining data with storytelling.

Acknowledgments

This book has been at least six years in the making. I didn't realise at the time, but it was sparked after delivering my first data storytelling workshop. As I continued to facilitate workshops, I found myself refining the content to better reflect the needs of those attending. **Thank you to everyone who has attended or supported one of my data storytelling workshops.** You have helped shape the content of this book.

Creating the book was definitely *not* a one-woman process. It took the help of a village to create. Here are some of the amazing people in my book-writing village.

Mark, one of my favourite people, thank you for all of your positivity and giving me the support I needed to do this.

Hayden, the biggest star in my universe, thank you for reading this book cover-to-cover and highlighting the parts you didn't understand. Not many 12-year-olds would have persevered, but you've helped make this book easier for others to understand (and for me to create the glossary).

Ameesha Green and **The Book Shelf team**, this book wouldn't have happened without your book-writing advice and guidance. Thank you!

Thabata Romanowski and **Steven Youngblood**, you each helped me unpack challenging concepts. Thank you for your insights and for being my personal cheerleaders.

Cole Nussbaumer Knaflic, thank you for not only creating the path that led me into this field but also for supporting my journey on it. I'm honoured you wrote the book's foreword.

Andy Kirk, **Brent Dykes**, and **Randy Olson**, you all continue to inspire me with the work you do. Thank you for your support and kind words to include as part of this book.

Alberto Cairo, thank you for providing invaluable initial feedback and calling out my curse of knowledge.

RJ Andrews, thank you for advising me to lean into what makes me unique. The New Zealand birds are due to you.

Kallie Bailey, thank you for our daily musings on the highs and lows of book writing and life.

Shane Gibson, thank you for giving me the kick I needed to pick up this book-writing thing again.

My amazing beta readers, thank you. I have been incredibly humbled by how generous you've been with your time and how considerate your feedback was. I enjoyed your different perspectives, which have helped make this book better than I could have ever achieved alone. With my deepest appreciation, thank you very much.

Aaron Schiff, Abhinav Malasi, Alexander Waleczek, Alexandra Hartman, Angie Melissa Morales Avella, Claire Wouts, Daniel Reed, Esther Voituron, Gabriel Belo Lima, Geoff Hunt, Imalka Jayalath, Jeff Barlow-Spady, Kalina Georgettes, Kate Kolich, Kelly Roehm, Koyel Chakraborty, Marita Hastings, Martin Vibrans, Mayuri L, Michael Von Geldern, Michelle Bidwell, Michelle Tjondro, Natalie Smith, Neil Richards, Nigel Hawtin, Opeyemi Jagunmolu, Qusay Sunjoq, Rachel Foong, Ricardo Rodriguez Ph.D., Robert Crocker, Ryan Huynh, Salomé Serieys, Sarah D. Massengill, Shaun McGirr, Sophie Burgess, Sophie Ferrlein, Steve Carline, Steven Youngblood, Swati Bharani, Tania Jury-Field, Thabata Romanowski, Tim Osborn, Todd Nicholson, Tom Shanley, Troy Kusabs, Vijay Thiruvengadam, Vince McSkimmings, and **Zoe Hindle.**

And lastly, for reasons too big to name, thank you to my **mum** (who now understands what I do), my **dad, Newa,** and **Alan.**

Template Downloads

The templates introduced in this book can be downloaded at roguepenguin.co.nz/book/downloads

- **Business Goal Hierarchy**

- **Problem-Goal-Action-Impact (PGAI) Framework**

- **Stakeholder Matrix**

- **Empathy Spectrums**

- **Time Data Story Canvas**

- **Character Data Story Canvas**

Glossary

ABT Framework
An approach to advance a story through its three acts using the words AND, BUT, and THEREFORE (or their synonyms).

ABT statement
A sentence or paragraph used in the ABT Framework.

A/B test
A method used to compare two different versions of something to see which one performs better.

Analyst
A person who analyses data.

Annotations
Comments or explanations that are added to a data visual to provide additional information or context.

Business acumen
The ability to understand and apply knowledge about business operations.

Business goal hierarchy
A structured representation of a business's goals, arranged in a hierarchical fashion to illustrate the relationships and dependencies between them.

Character
Whoever (or whatever) the data story is about.

Chromatic colours
All shades except for black, white, and their mixture, grey (these are known as **achromatic colours**).

Customer churn rate
The rate at which customers stop doing business with a company, typically measured over a specific period.

Customer churn model
An analytical tool to forecast and understand the likelihood of customers discontinuing their use of a product or service.

Dashboard
A visual display or user interface that presents important information and data in a consolidated and easily accessible format, typically using **Inform** visuals.

Data analytics (also known as data analysis)
The process of examining, cleaning, transforming, visualising, and interpreting data to discover data insights.

Data insight
Knowledge gained from analysing data.

Data literacy
Someone's ability to read and interpret data.

Data measurement
The specific data value of a data metric.

Data metric
Something that can be measured.

Data story
A narrative that communicates a data-derived message.

Data story building blocks
Specific pieces of information that can be used to create a data story.

Data Story Canvas
A template organising the data story building blocks. *Time* and *Character* data stories have a slightly different canvas.

Data storytelling
The process of communicating a data-derived message. This can also refer to the final output of this process.

Data visualisation
The process of presenting data visually. This can also refer to the final output of this process (also known as a **data visual**).

Discover visual
A data visual used by an analyst to discover data insight.

Educate visual
A data visual used by a knowledge-seeking audience to understand the meaning of data insights.

Expression
A sentence created by combining the Time(s), Character(s), Data Metric, and Data Change/Difference building blocks.

Inform visual
A data visual used by a subject expert to easily access data measurements.

Key performance indicator (KPI)
A data metric used to show how part of a business is doing.

Lifetime value (LTV)
The total expected revenue a business can generate from a single customer over the entire duration of their relationship.

Nested data story
A data story written to provide more detail on a specific part of a more summarised data story.

Net profit
The amount of money a business has left after deducting all of its expenses.

PGAI Framework
An approach to define your business reason to create a data story, including the problem you're hoping to solve, your goal, action taken, and impact created.

Sentiment analysis
A process that identifies and categorises the emotional tone (positive, negative, or neutral) conveyed by text.

Stakeholder Matrix
A visual tool that categorises audience groups based on their level of interest and influence in a project.

Stakeholders
Individuals or groups that have an interest, concern, or "stake" in a particular project, business, or endeavour.

Summary data story
A data story written at its highest level.

Three-act story structure
A story structure consisting of three parts (agreement, contrast, and consequence).

Made in the USA
Columbia, SC
22 November 2024

47325964R00223